PRESIDENT BRYAN

A PIONEER COLLEGE

AND

ITS BACKGROUND

(THE OHIO UNIVERSITY)

By CHARLES WILLIAM SUPER

"In the senate of the immortals, in the temple of the dead, the only voice worthy to break the silence is the voice of truth."

γεγήρασκα διδασκόμενος καὶ διδάσκων.—*Solon*
(*I have grown old learning and teaching.*)

1924
NEWCOMB & GAUSS, *Printers*
SALEM, MASS.

To

ELMER BURRITT BRYAN

president of the Ohio University

this volume is inscribed by one who,

while never claiming to be an educator,

may rightfully claim a place among old

school and college men, if not among

"gentlemen of the old school"

PREFACE

THIS unpretentious volume is not so much a history as it is an interpretation. It is an endeavor to fathom motives no less than to record events. It is certainly neither a eulogy nor a panegyric. The author who places before his readers half truths for whole truths, or whole truths in a false light, is a public malefactor. Every man should be shown while he yet lives that you cannot transform a radical sinner into a radiant saint simply by putting his corpse in a coffin. Although the narrator of these events makes no claim to the somewhat familiar

*horum magna pars fui,**

he does not hesitate to appropriate the latter half of the quotation. He affirms that he has written objectively, but he does not deny that he has now and then been influenced by the Horatian dictum

ridentem dicere verum
Quid vetat?†

The prophet Elijah was a very serious-minded person, yet it is a matter of record that at least once in his lifetime he made some speeches that were a mixture of irony and sarcasm. Although the O. U. was not only, for several decades, a small college but one of the smallest in the State, it was by no means insignificant. Neither was Athens without its influence even in national affairs and politics. Both have proved the truth of the proverb that it does not depend on the size or a cow could catch a rabbit. And as for beauty, is not the canary a

* "A major part of which I was."
† "If a man tells the truth with a smile, who should forbid?"

PREFACE

handsomer bird than even the American eagle? Although the river that flows by Athens is a small stream, its water is as wet as that of the Ohio or even of the Mississippi and is not often so dirty. Moreover, the government of the local college was probably unique and is so still. The president of the college is also president of the board of trustees. This arrangement, while not without its drawbacks, is doubtless the best that could be made. Everything or almost everything depends upon the mentality of the person who occupies the double office. The writer of this sketch has had the opportunity to see its workings from three points of view: from that of the students, or rather, from that of students, from that of the faculty and from that of the trustees. He learned not only what they did, but also what some of them proposed to do or all left undone.

CHARLES WILLIAM SUPER.

Athens, Ohio, March 31, 1924.

EXPLANATORY NOTE

THE sources from which the data used in the compilation of this volume have been drawn are generally mentioned in the course of the narrative. Among the more comprehensive works Charles M. Walker's "History of Athens County" is a reliable guide. But as it was published in 1869 it contains no matter pertaining to its subject for more than half a century. Professor Martzloff, late of the college faculty, had stored in his memory and in manuscripts a mass of information bearing on the history of his native State, which he placed freely and generously at my disposal. The writer deeply regrets that his death in 1922 made his counsel no longer available. A volume dealing mainly with the legal phase of the subject is "A Legal History of the Ohio University" by W. E. Peters of the Athens bar. The more recent volume by the same author, "Ohio Lands and Their Subdivisions," is hardly less illuminating. It sheds so much light on the whole problem of land-grants, probably the most important of all the problems suggested by the familiar line:

"Westward the star of empire takes its way,"

that every Ohioan who is interested in the development of his native State should not only read the book but should familiarize himself with its contents. Considerable data have been obtained by correspondence and from oral testimony. On the other hand, my efforts to get information in this way were not in all cases conducive to equanimity of mind and placidity of temper. Some of my let-

EXPLANATORY NOTE

ters were treated with neglect and answered with silence. The thought that while genius has its limitations stupidity has not, failed to convince me that an act of boorishness is always to be excused with the reflection that "some people are born that way." For the general make-up of the volume the author is solely responsible.

THE OHIO UNIVERSITY AND
ITS BACKGROUND

I

THE historian of movements or of institutions,
whether they be political, religious or social, is almost sure to mislead his readers if he does not take
into consideration preceding and contemporary
conditions. We are so prone to project the present
into the past, to see with our eyes instead of with
the constructive imagination, that unless we are
constantly on our guard we shall misunderstand
and misinterpret the days gone by. The history of
the O. U. (this abbreviation will henceforth be
employed in order to save space), the earliest venture into the domain in higher education in the
Northwest, is an instructive example of what has
just been written. When viewed in the light of
present conditions we are prompted to believe that
the project was launched either by a company of
school boys who had a totally inadequate conception
of what they were doing, or by men whose enthusiasm far outran their judgment. But when con-
templated in the light of the closing years of the
eighteenth century it was altogether rational and
wisely conceived. It was one of the first land-grant
colleges, if not the first, and if its property had
been administered as its founders intended it should
be and expected it would be, its income would have
been far larger proportionately than accrued from
the Morrill bill enacted more than half a century
later.

[1]

A PIONEER COLLEGE

The moral and intellectual forces that led to the founding of a college in a territory in which there were as yet no white settlers were generated and developed in New England, mainly in Connecticut. The specific form in which the enterprise took shape was mainly due to a man who was a graduate of Yale College. On the other hand the conception seems to have had its origin in the mind of a man who had no systematic education and who was entirely self-taught, namely Rufus Putnam. As Yale was the spiritual father of the O. U., let us consider for a moment its origin and the sort of education it provided when Manasseh Cutler was a young man. It seems to have had no legal name until 1745 and no fixed abiding-place although it began teaching in a small way ten years earlier. In 1718 Elihu Yale contributed money and property to the value of some hundreds of pounds to the infant enterprise and the trustees gave the name "Yale" to the building they were then erecting in New Haven. The appellation seems to have been a sort of afterthought. It was, however, applied to the college itself, but the charter dates only from 1745. The Yale building was one hundred and seventy feet long, of proportionate width and three stories high, with an attic. It was used as a chapel, dining-room, library and residence hall. It was the custom of college authorities to provide lodgings for students, until after the middle of the nineteenth century and has not even yet been entirely discontinued. No inconsiderable income was derived from this source. For three decades the Yale building, which was of wood, seems to have served its purpose and to have been sufficiently commodious. By the

[2]

end of this period it had become a good deal dilapidated and was torn down. As young Cutler was an undergraduate during this period we have a fair record of his student life and also of the studies he pursued. I do not find any report of the number of his fellow students but it can hardly have been so many as a hundred. Connecticut was at that time much more sparsely settled than Massachusetts and it was a rare event for a student to go far from home to attend school in those early days. In 1637 the population was about 1800. Fifty years later it had increased tenfold. In 1755 it was 133,000, of which number 3500 were slaves. In 1787 the population was about 200,000. Nathan Hale was a member of the class of 1773 at Yale. In 1800 the students numbered two hundred and seventeen. Among them were many from the South. That the pro-slavery sentiment long perdured in Connecticut was demonstrated by the fierce persecution to which Miss Crandall was subjected when she admitted a colored girl into her school. Among other things her house was set on fire. John C. Calhoun, a man whose whole private life was without reproach, graduated at Yale in 1804 and afterwards studied law at Litchfield for three years. The difficulties of travel also had much to do with the founding of colleges including the so-called academies in those days. Rarely has a man reaped so much glory from so small an investment as Elihu Yale. He does not seem to have been a resident of New England at any time, in the strict sense of the term; nor does Jeremiah Dummer, a native of Boston and a graduate of Harvard, who appears to have been chiefly instrumental in securing the initial donation from Yale. It was small compared with his wealth. Since then nowhere in the world has so much been done for higher education by private beneficence as in the United States. The collegiate school, the predecessor of Yale College, appears to have sojourned temporarily at no less than six different places and at two different towns at the same time for a short period. The War of the Revolution was a disturbing factor more than once. Latin was prescribed as the principal medium of conversation, but we are not informed how regularly the prescription was taken. This was the custom at the German gymnasia at the same time and long afterwards. Until many years later all, and then most of the lectures at the German universities were delivered in Latin. It does not appear that Latin was ever used as a medium of instruction either in Great Britain or in this country. Except in the professional schools, instruction was almost wholly by recitations from a text-book. Charles F. Thwing in his "History of Education in America," furnishes some interesting statistics regarding the subjects studied at Yale in the eighteenth century. In 1733 Euclid became the text-book in geometry. In 1742 elementary mathematics was placed at the beginning instead of at the end of the course, where it had hitherto been. In 1763, two years before Manasseh Cutler received his degree, algebra was first introduced. In 1777 the Freshmen studied arithmetic, the Sophomores algebra and geometry, the Juniors trigonometry. In 1734, thirty-seven pounds were collected and invested in the purchase of apparatus. Although Nathan Hale, who was executed as a spy in 1776, received his degree eight

[4]

years after Cutler, the course was almost precisely the same.*

The first professorship of chemistry at Harvard was established in 1791, but no laboratory was provided. Beginning about 1847, a few students received instruction in chemistry from Professor Horsford at the Lawrence Scientific School. Not many years later, C. W. Eliot was given the freedom of Professor J. P. Cooke's laboratory and made good use of its facilities. When he became president of his *alma mater* he interested himself particularly in this department.

The first professor at Dickinson was Thomas Cooper, an Oxonian and friend of Joseph Priestley, the discoverer of oxygen. He held the position from 1811 to 1815. For many years chemistry and physics were taught by the same man at the college and considerable apparatus was accumulated. But

---

* In a recently discovered diary for the year 1776 kept by Abraham ten Broeck, a member of the New York General Assembly and now in possession of Mr. J. N. Barry of Portland, Oregon, it is recorded that Philadelphia with a population of forty thousand was "supposed to be the largest and most regularly laid out city in North America. It contains forty thousand people." Also "a great number of church buildings." Charleston, S. C., is credited with a population of fifteen thousand. New Jersey had no towns of any importance. New York College had "Professors in the different Branches of Science usually taught in European colleges." The building was only one third complete. "A Porter constantly attends at the Front gate which is locked at ten o'clock each Evening in Summer and at nine in Winter; after which Hours the names of those that come in are delivered weekly to the President." The College and Academy of Philadelphia included a grammar school and charity schools for boys and girls. Expense of Boarding, Washing, Lodging and Firewood were about seventy-six dollars per annum. "Nassau Hall at Prince-town is handsome and commodious." Yale college has two professors and two tutors. Rhode Island College had thirty-five students and the grammar school eighteen. "The college edifice is a fine building."

[5]

for a long time the lessons were oral and the demonstrations ocular, few of the students taking part in the manipulations.

The difference in the religious points of view between the founders of Yale and Harvard is of peculiar interest. In the petition laid before the legislature praying for the incorporation of the college it was set forth as one of the objects "the upholding of the Protestant religion without any narrowing or sectarian qualifications." When the college was incorporated it was endowed with an annual grant of money equal to about sixty pounds. Elihu Yale while in England, whither he had been sent by his father to be educated, became a member of the Anglican church. Yet we should be on our guard against attriuting much importance to these paper conditions. For, as Doyle remarks in his "Colonies under the House of Hanover," "Although Yale was in some measure a monument of the moderate and liberal temper of Connecticut, its early history serves also to illustrate that process of reaction by which Massachusetts was becoming the home of theological freedom; Connecticut, that of dogmatic orthodoxy. In spite of the Anglican associations connected with Yale college, it is clear that many of the strictly orthodox Calvinists of Massachusetts sympathized with and supported the foundation of a society likely to be an effective rival to Harvard. Personal feeling, we may be sure, contributed to this. The exclusion of Increase Mather from the headship of Harvard not only called into the field the persistent and clamorous hostility of his son, but had no doubt alarmed many in whose eyes the ejected president represented the best of the New territory. They did their part in enticing the people westward. An English traveller in the United States at the end of the first decade of the nineteenth century was informed that in eighteen months, fifteen thousand wagons bearing emigrants had passed over one bridge in New York. Another traveler about the same time mentions a singular party of emigrants—a man, his wife and ten children. "The youngest of his progeny tied on his back, the father pushed a wheelbarrow containing the movables of the family." They had come from New Jersey and their destination was Ohio. One family of eight walked from Maine to Pennsylvania drawing goods and children in a handcart. Farther on the way a woman is passed carrying a baby on her arms and leading a child by the hand. By 1814 the poor were deserting the East in such numbers as to arouse fears that it would become depopulated. There were also many deserted farms in Virginia. People left that State so rapidly that the legislature at one time seriously considered the advisability of taking some action to check the exodus. Many of these people were rough and rugged, but they were in the minority. The proportion of "lewd fellows of the baser sort," at least in Ohio, was never large. We meet almost everywhere the influence of the itinerant preachers of which mention has been made more than once in this volume. Peter Cartwright, a popular preacher of the Methodist persuasion, served two terms in the Illinois legislature and was an unsuccessful candidate for congress against Abraham Lincoln. Here is what Mr. Walker has to say, in his "History of Athens county," about one of the early land deals, that at

England orthodoxy and learning. Yet over and above this, it is clear that the supposed laxity of religious teaching at Harvard was an important element in the new movement." In 1701 President Mather of Harvard was superseded by Samuel Willard. Mather's son Cotton entered Harvard at the age of twelve (1675) and was later involved in the Salem witchcraft delusion.

Dr. Wheelock was the first president of Dartmouth College after its removal from Lebanon. The college was a concrete expression of sympathy for the Indians, which was a characteristic of New England philanthropy for more than a century after the first settlement of the region. Although the Indian portion of the project never amounted to anything, it was not altogether abandoned until 1849. From its inception it was a well-meant but mistaken policy. The endeavor to educate the Red Man in a "college" is instructive as showing the meaning attached to the term in those days. When Williams College began operations in 1793, it had a building, a few books and funds amounting to about nine thousand dollars. There was but one chair for the two ancient languages until 1853. The number of students on hand at any one time to the close of the century seems not to have exceeded twenty-five. It was hardly more than an offshoot of Yale. It was at this college that W. C. Bryant, who was born in the year of its establishment, spent a few terms after he was sixteen. When Timothy Dwight became president of Yale in 1795, the faculty consisted of one professor and three tutors, while the number of students did not much exceed a hundred. There was no chair of any language until

DR. EDWIN WATTS CHUBB
Dean of the College of Liberal Arts

A PIONEER COLLEGE

II

Having thus cast a fleeting glance over the
moter educational background of the Ohio Univ
sity, it will be in order to consider briefly the l
that drew a large number of families from
settled regions east of the Hudson and the De
ware to the wilds that began on the western a
northern banks of the Ohio River. One was t
fertility of the soil compared with that of N
England. But the attraction in front was aided
the repulsion in the rear. The revolution had l
many people worse off than it found them.
fact, it was not a movement from beneath but fr
above. It was in a large measure a struggle b
tween the well-to-do in Great Britain and the sa
class in the colonies. The slogan, "No taxatio
without representation" can be interpreted in var
ous senses, and is even now much misunderstood.
it any more unjust than "Taxation in spite of repr
sentation"? When the poor, usually landles
learned of the boundless domain that began only
few miles to the west they made their way thithe
by any means within their compass. The firs
settlers in Ohio and farther west usually reache
the river of the same name at some point betwee
Pittsburg and its mouth; then made their way to o
towards their destination by the force of the cur
rent; then up the smaller streams by the force o
muscle. The first capital of Indiana, Corydon, wa
only a few miles from the Ohio River. The clas
of men later known as land-sharks, land-grabbers
and land-pirates were active all over the western

[9]

Gallipolis in Gallia county (both names are signifi-
cant). The county seat of Gallia county is about
fifty miles south of Athens. "The confused and
mysterious accounts cannot, even at this distance of
time, be read without a lively pity for the sufferings
of the poor Frenchmen and indignation at the
authors of their misfortunes. With this, however,
neither Dr. Cutler nor the Ohio company had anything to do. Their action was all in good faith."
But did not these "authors" all belong to the
"Fathers" of whose virtues we read and hear so
much?

The other attraction was the Ordinance of 1787.
This document, which has been much praised, often
over-praised, was in some respects in advance of
the age, as there was at that date no Constitution
of the United States because there was no United
States. In others, it was not only conservative but
would now be considered decidedly reactionary.
Like many other ordinances, laws and decrees, it
was easier to put on paper than to put in force. We
need to consider here only a few of its important
points. "Religion, morality and knowledge, being
necessary to good government, schools and the
means of education shall forever be encouraged.
The utmost good faith shall always be observed
towards the Indians, their lands and property shall
never be taken from them without their consent;
and their property rights and liberty shall never be
invaded or disturbed, unless in just and lawful wars
authorized by Congress." "There shall be neither
slavery nor involuntary servitude, otherwise than in
punishment of crimes whereof the parties shall have
been duly convicted." On the other hand, the ordi-

[11]

nance recognized property not only as a qualification for holding office but even for voting. It provided that the governor of the Territory must be the owner of one thousand acres of land, while other officials must be the owners of from five hundred to two hundred acres. The possessor of less than fifty acres was disfranchised. Although the document prohibited slavery—or rather forbade it—the prohibition was for many years a dead letter. No part of the entire territory was free soil, although Ohio came nearest to fulfilling this condition. From East Liverpool to Cairo there was only the Ohio River between prospective freedom and actual slavery but not many of those who crossed the river had human property to take with them. A few had and did not leave it behind. There was no one to say them nay. There were, in what was once "Territory," a few slaves as late as 1847—illegally, of course. But they probably had no desire to escape, as slaves in the North, at least after the adoption of the Constitution, were regarded as house servants or hired hands rather than property. So recently as 1830 there were not far from one hundred slaves in the Keystone State. Doubtless the chief reason why African slavery perdured so long was that the blacks never made any serious or concerted effort to gain their own freedom. They did not realize that God helps those who help themselves. They are naturally docile, perhaps even servile in disposition. All attempts to enslave the Indians were futile. It is a curious historical fact that it was white men who not only freed the slaves but taught them that they had a right to freedom. Both General Harrison and General Grant are said to have owned slaves. It will not be easy for those who were born after about 1865 or who may yet be born, to understand how little opposition there was up to that time, or at least to the middle of the century, to an institution that is now almost universally condemned and even execrated. It was the determination on the part of the Southern leaders to rend the Union in twain that precipitated the bloody conflict. The constitution of Ohio did not give the colored man the ballot until a few years ago. The absurdity involved in the action of the people in withholding the ballot would be incredible, if anything in human conduct were incredible, after the adoption of the Fifteenth Amendment to the Federal Constitution. It is probable also that in the States formed from the Northwest Territory slaves were rarely or never sold or bought. In a country where the great majority of the people were desperately poor, the negro slave could not be poorer and he had no taxes to pay. It will also be in order, in this connection, to put the unsophisticated reader on his guard against two errors into which he is likely to fall when reading the early history of the United States. He should keep in mind the fact that American slavery up to about 1830 was a very different institution from what it was after about that date. Our narrative shows that men passed freely from North to South and from South to North without the slightest feeling that they were going among aliens or strangers. The other error into which it is almost or quite impossible to avoid falling is to form a correct estimate of the purchasing power of money at different periods even in the same country and under the same form of government. Mere figures mean hardly anything. In the early days very small amounts of cash were sufficient; very little was indispensable except for the payment of taxes and a few cents now and then for the payment of postage.*

Although the Ohio Conference of the Methodist Episcopal Church included territory not in Ohio, the proceedings of said body, when it met in Chillicothe in October, 1812, makes it clear that there were slaves in the State. It was resolved, among other things, that "No member of our Society shall purchase a slave except in cases of humanity or mercy to the slave purchased, and if he purchase a slave or slaves, he shall state to the next meeting of the Quarterly Conference the number of years he thinks the slave or slaves should serve as a compensation for the price paid," etc. It was also stipulated that "if any member of our Society shall sell a slave except at the request of the slave to prevent separation of families, he shall be excluded from the Society," etc.

---

* The Ohio Company's Purchase contains one proviso that is probably unique in all similar transactions. It set aside one tract of land, or rather, a portion of their tract, the money realized from the sales of which was to be used for the support of religion, meaning, of course, the Christian religion. A similar reservation was made in the case of the Symmes purchase, on which Miami University is located. With the completion of these two sales the government ceased making such donations. Although many efforts were subsequently made, Congress took little heed of them. The last and final appeal was brought before the Federal legislature in 1811, when the Baptist denomination of Salem, Miss., was granted the use of five acres on which it had built a church. But President Monroe vetoed the act on the ground that it was in conflict with that amendment to the constitution which stipulated that "Congress shall make no law respecting the establishment of religion," etc. As the bill could not be passed over the President's veto, no further efforts were made in the same direction.—Peters.

Although the membership of the Conference was reported to be nearly twenty-three thousand, of the sixty preachers whose names appear on the minutes, more than half had deficiencies in their salaries. Yet the salary for a single man was only eighty dollars and for a married man twice this sum. And there were twenty-two married men. The war that broke out the same year made conditions worse than they were before and we find numerous complaints of outrageous profiteering, although this word was not in use at that date. It is also part of the record that some of the "brethren" were among the worst offenders.

Eight years later the Conference met again at Chillicothe. Of the preachers only three had received more than two hundred dollars, a few having received less than fifty dollars. What a spirit of self-sacrifice and devotion to duty shine forth from the background of the Ohio University!

It is almost impossible for those of us who believe with John Wesley that slavery is the sum of all villainies to form a just estimate of American public opinion regarding the institution until far along in the eighteenth century. As slavery forms an important fact in the early history of American institutions it may be well to give in this connection a few additional data. Here are some quotations bearing on the question to be found in a volume entitled "Truths of History," written by Mildred Rutherford and published at Athens, Ga. All quotation marks are omitted except where they are used by the author. Abraham Lincoln was not in any sense an Abolitionist. He had no intention to make voters of negroes—in fact, their welfare did

III

It is also at least worthy of passing mention that Ohio, although the first portion of the new territory to be settled, was not the first to be occupied. The French laid claim to a large part thereof. Lasalle was the chief explorer. Neither was the Ordinance the first official document granting complete religious liberty in the United States. In this matter it was preceded by New York, by Pennsylvania, and perhaps by other States and even colonies. There seems no doubt that with the admission of Ohio a definite and general policy for promoting education by the general government was entered upon. When Indiana, Mississippi, Illinois and Alabama were admitted into the Union, bargains and grants similar to that already existing were made and given. The grants were not, however, all of the same type. The total amounted to about eighty million acres which, at the original valuation of about one dollar and twenty-five cents an acre, would have yielded one hundred million dollars. Most of the grants were, however, grossly mismanaged, sometimes ignorantly, sometimes fraudulently. By the compact entered into with Samuel Osgood, Manasseh Cutler, Arthur Lee and Winthrop Sargent on behalf of the Ohio Company on the one hand and the Board of Treasury on the other, there being at that time no Federal Executive, it was stipulated that two townships of land should be given or set apart in perpetuity for an university. The transaction bears date October 27, 1787. We are not here further concerned with it except to note that the lands were to be appraised at about one dollar and seventy-five cents an acre and to be reappraised three times in a century. It would seem from such evidence as is obtainable at this date that the lands were taken up with considerable rapidity and that the two townships were entirely under lease by 1820. As the period of the first reappraisement approached, the trustees of the college, at the suggestion of president McGuffey, had incurred debts to an amount mentioned elsewhere in this book, not doubting that such reappraisement could and would be made. That this confidence was justified was proved by a committee of the General Assembly and by several decisions of the courts. But this was one of the schemes that was destined to "gang agley." The hostility of the lessees is incimprehensible to the present generation. So unpopular had president McGuffey made himself by his efforts in behalf of the college that he was subjected to personal violence although not of a serious character, and even hanged in effigy. The law which may be said to have asphyxiated the institution for a number of years was passed on the tenth day of March, 1843, and reads as follows: "Be it enacted by the General Assembly of the State of Ohio, That the true intent and meaning of the first section of the act entitled 'An act establishing an university in the town of Athens,' passed February twenty-first, 1805, that the leases granted and by virtue of said act, and the one to which that was an amendment, should not be subject to revaluation at any time thereafter as was provided for in the act to which that was an amendment." The peculiarity of this of this addition to the rent on the original leases. On the other hand, it would seem to be a self-evident proposition that the exemption from the payment of a State tax was made, not in the interest of the payer but of the payee. Besides, entirely apart from the merits of the case, the presence of a college in a community or its proximity thereto, is always a paying proposition, if nothing else. As the entire income of the college, under the terms of the original appraisement, was only about forty-five hundred dollars, we see what ideas the lessees and a majority of the legislators had as to the amount of money required to carry on an institution of higher learning. The rent equal to the State tax which, under the terms of the decision just mentioned, the lessees were required to pay increased this amount by almost fifty percent, as has just been pointed out. The land values of the two townships, including the railroad beds for the year 1919, was nearly two million dollars. Although this sum at six per cent would yield a much larger income than Dr. Cutler believed to be necessary for the maintenance of the university, it is not only small when compared with the actual budget, but with the needs, real or imaginary, of such an institution. According to the treasurer's report for the year ending June 20, 1920, the total expenditures of the O. U. were in excess of three hundred and thirty thousand dollars. This sum, moreover, does not include the money spent by the students on private account, which was probably not much, if any, less. It would seem that a person of even very limited intelligence could see, without any special effort, on which side of the balance sheet the profits would

[22]

lie. But, as has been said before, the people of the nineteenth century cannot be greatly blamed if they did not look far into the future. A demonstration is always more convincing than a prediction.*

* In an important case that was brought before the supreme court of Pennsylvania in "the early days," Judge Gibson decided that "If anything is self-evident in the structure of our government, it is that the legislature has no power to order a new trial either before or after judgment. The power of the legislature is not judicial. It is limited to the making of laws, not to the exposition or execution of them."

IV

In 1881 the college experienced another slight
check. In March of said year the General Assembly passed an act appropriating twenty thousand
dollars to be used in repairing its buildings. Forthwith certain members of the Senate who had vigorously opposed this grant, obtained an injunction on
the State treasurer to estop him from paying this
money to the treasurer of the college. After a short
delay the injunction was dissolved and a peremp-
tory writ in favor of the trustees ordered. This
appropriation was later increased by ten thousand
dollars. Part of it was used in the construction of
what was long known as the "old chapel." In 1883
another crisis in the affairs of the university may be
said to have arisen, when President Scott was called
to the head of the State University at Columbus.
The trustees held several meetings and correspond-
ed with two or more prospective candidates for the
vacancy. All declined on account of the uncertainty
of the future. During this interregnum a bill was
introduced in the legislature with a view to uniting
the three States Universities under one management, to be called the University of Ohio. But the
centralizing tendency which it seemed to encourage
met with so much opposition that the project was
never pushed. In this regard the policy of the
States varies. Some of the older States have virtually no State University. Others have but a single
institution so named. Others have two or more that
are supposed to stand on an equal footing. Ohio

DR. IRMA E. VOIGT
Dean of the College of Women

has now at least three universities supported by taxation and two municipal universities. Previous to
the spring of 1885 the general assembly had made
no appropriation to the O. U. for current expenses.
However, to the surprise and gratification of its
friends, the legislature accepted an amendment to
the general appropriation bill granting about five
thousand dollars for this purpose. Dr. Richard-
son, at the time superintendent of the Athens asy-
lum for the insane, although not a trustee, aided
materially in bringing about this result. Small as
the amount was, it prepared the way for larger
sums in the future. The following year the legislature granted five thousand dollars for the establishment of a "normal department." This was the
first appropriation for such a purpose made by an
Ohio general assembly. The item was also bitterly
contested and was kept in the appropriation bill by
a bare majority. Its most vigorous champion was
the Hon. W. S. Matthews who had been a student
for a short time after the close of the sectional war.
The rejuvenation of the O. U. may be said to date
from the enactment, by the general assembly, of
what is locally known as the Sleeper Bill from the
Hon. D. L. Sleeper, the member from Athens
county and Speaker of the House. By a fortunate
concatenation of circumstances, the senator from
the district to which Athens County belonged was
also a resident of Athens. The essential part of the
law which was passed in 1896 is that "there shall be
levied annually a tax on the grand duplicate of the
taxable property of Ohio . . . three one-hun-
dredths of a mill upon each dollar of valuation of
such taxable property. Of the funds thus collected

seven-twelfths are to be paid to the treasurer of the Ohio University and five-twelfths to the treasurer of the Miami University." Although the sum at first realized by the two institutions was not large, being only about fifty-seven thousand dollars, the act virtually committed the State Legislature to their support. This support has not since been withheld, and has been increasingly liberal, as has already been pointed out. Howbeit, one would hardly be accused of exaggeration if he were to affirm that during a large part of the nineteenth century the trustees were either inside the fort defending it against enemy onslaughts or on the outside trying to collect the tribute which they claimed was justly their due. Not only is it a truth of wide application that eternal vigilance is the price of liberty, it is certainly true in this case that unremitting watchfulness was necessary to prevent the "hostiles" from destroying the university, or reducing it to its lowest terms. Leading citizens went so far in their hostility as to declare that the buildings ought to be burned down; and while these men probably would not have applied the torch themselves, they would not have been grieved nor have come to the rescue if some one else had done the deed. The college treasurer also received letters written in a disguised hand, warning him against trying to collect the additional rent granted by the Act of 1876. This rent amounted to less than five cents an acre, while on town property it was a mere trifle. Unfortunately, this dreary and disgraceful record is not unique. It could probably be paralleled by not a few educational institutions in the United States. If, as Virgil declares, it was a vast work—in modern parlance, a "big job" —to found the Roman nation, it was hardly less vast to establish a system of education both higher and lower in many of our States, if not in all.*

In 1900 both the senator from the district and the representative in the legislature were citizens of Athens, the former being a nephew of Bishop Moore and bearing the same name. He was also chosen a member of the finance committee. In March, 1902, the legislature passed what was known as the Seese law and which was virtually a replica of the Sleeper Bill. Its purpose was to establish and maintain a normal school "coordinate with the existing courses of instruction in such a state of efficiency as to provide proper theoretical and practical training for all students desiring to prepare themselves for the work of teaching." This act provided what is known as the Ohio and Miami University Fund by levying a tax of one-thirtieth of a mill on the taxable property of the State, the proceeds to be divided in the same proportion as under the Sleeper Bill. By a law passed in 1906 the sum was slightly increased and the amount realized from this source is now in excess of thirty-three thousand for the older institution. What is known as the Fouts Bill was enacted into a law in May, 1921. The author had been a student at the O.U. about a quarter of a century earlier and was at the time the Representative in the legislature from

* Regarding the two names proposed, see W. E. Peters in the volume referred to elsewhere, first part of chapter xv and post. page iii. "Valuation and revaluation" are dealt with in chapter xii. The reader may be prompted to ask why the lessees should object to a revaluation every twenty, sixty and ninety years, when in later times revaluation was made at much shorter periods all over the state.

[27]

Morgan county. By the provisions of said bill there was to be levied on the taxable property of the State a tax of twenty-five hundredths of a mill on the dollar, which tax shall be outside the tax limits prescribed by law. The object of this law was to create an educational building fund, which fund was to be distributed in the proportion of fourteen per cent for the O. U., fourteen per cent for Miami University and seventy-two per cent for the State University at Columbus. This law was to remain in effect for two years, only at the end of which period it lapses unless renewed. From this source the college will realize a sum not much less than four hundred thousand dollars.

Mr. Charles M. Walker, a member of the class of '53 and a native of Athens, uses language that is both veracious and vigorous when expressing his opinion of the shortsightedness of some of his neighbors in their hostility to the college. Being a man of education and culture, he saw farther into the future than those who lacked these qualifications. The following strictures may be found on pages 345-6 of his "History of Athens County." This volume, be it said in passing, is of a higher order than most of the so-called "county histories." "The pecuniary embarrassments of the university were so far overcome that its complete reorganization was accomplished in 1820, and in 1822 the faculty was constituted as follows: Rev. James Irvine, president and professor of mathematics; Joseph Dana, professor of languages; Rev. Jacob Lindley, professor of rhetoric and moral philosophy; Rev. Samuel D. Hoge, professor of natural science; and Henry D. Ward, academical preceptor. From this period may be dated the complete working system and large usefulness of the university. Literary societies had been organized some years before; the nuclei of three respectable libraries—a college library, a library of the Athenian, and one of the Philomathean literary society—had been formed, philosophical apparatus secured, a fine cabinet of minerals begun. The institution has had its times of prosperity and depression, but during the last half of the century it has, in the aggregate, accomplished noble results and sent forth from its halls a large number of men both able and active. At the present time the university is with difficulty sustained and its condition is no credit to the State. It has an able and faithful corps of instructors who, in spite of difficulties, are laboring, not without success. But the institution should have State aid. It was the design of the Ohio Company and the purpose of Congress to make it a nobly endowed university—the most nobly endowed at that time of any in the United States. But by mismanagement and trickery, it has been, through a series of years, cheated out of its revenues. It should have a large income from its original endowment, and that without in the least burdening the lessees of these lands. The State owes it to the founders of the university, who established it with prayers and difficulties such as we little comprehend, that it shall not permanently be kept out of its rights by legal technicalities and we cannot doubt that the people and the legislature will eventually come to this conclusion. It will be a disgrace to them, if the first university founded west of the Alleghanies and around which 'Memories cluster thick as flowers' shall be allowed to fall into decay and disappear for the want of the aid it has a right to expect and demand." The hope and the prediction expressed in these eloquent lines began to be fulfilled a few years after they were written and are still in process of fulfillment. It is enlightening, though not creditable that some one has written on the margin of one of the college copies of said history opposite the passage beginning "At the present time," this comment: "A damned lie." And, the handwriting indicates that it was not done by a naughty boy; it was the verdict of a local chirographer.

There is considerable available evidence to the effect that the children in the new environment grew up less intelligent and less interested in knowledge than their parents. Most of the latter had acquired something more than the rudiments of an education in the "East," although the term East must be somewhat liberally interpreted. They carried with them into the wilderness some of the books they owned. We also see from the autobiography of Thomas Ewing that they took infinite pains to increase their scanty store. When these books were lost or worn out they were often not replaced, if at all, until the means of transportation became better and printed matter became less costly. The origin and immediate ancestry of the early settlers in southern Ohio and perhaps also in other parts of the State had much influence on their attitude towards higher learning. This thought finds expression more than once in these pages because it obtrudes itself on the attention of the writer as he scans the early records.

V

Theodore Roosevelt, in his "Winning of the West," points out that western Pennsylvania was the great breeding ground for the earliest settlers who made their way into the valley of the Ohio. There were, however, among the immigrants into the new territory many from western Virginia, as I have stated in my sketch of Dickinson and also briefly in another part of this volume. These were mostly non-slaveholders who, after the adoption of the Ordinance of 1787, migrated into a land where slavery was outlawed. There were, however, among those Virginians some who took their slaves with them despite the Ordinance. The immigrants from the Keystone State were for the most part Presbyterians, which accounts for their prominence in the early history of the O. U. Among these pioneers was Jacob Lindley. He was born in Washington County, Pa., still a stronghold of Presbyterianism, in 1774. He graduated at Princeton in 1800. He was licensed to preach by the Washington Presbytery and in 1803 removed to Ohio where he was installed as pastor of a church at Waterford, a township and village on the Muskingum River, about twenty miles from its mouth. The village long ago attained the point of stable equilibrium with a population of about fifteen score of inhabitants. A few years later Mr. Lindley was appointed a trustee of the Ohio University, although there was at the time no such institution visible. This position he held until his removal to the South in 1838. When the preparatory department of the college was organized Mr. Lindley was appointed preceptor and also president of the board of trustees. The trustees appointed in 1804 were (1) Elijah Backus, (2) General Rufus Putnam, (3) Hon. Dudley Woodbridge, (4) Hon. Benjamin Tappan, (5) Bazaleel Wells, (6) General Nathaniel Massie, (7) Hon. Daniel Symmes, (8) Rev. Daniel Story, (9) Samuel Carpenter, (10) Rev. James Kilbourn, (11) Griffin Greene, Sr., and (12) Joseph Darlington. Of these appointees 4, 5, 6, 7, and 11 never acted. The two clergymen were residents of Marietta. In 1805 Hon. William Creighton, Gen. Joseph Buell, Benjamin Tupper, Rev. Jacob Lindley, and Michael Baldwin were appointed. The first and last named also never acted. The president of the college was usually also president of the board, but not always. For several years, so far as the college was concerned, Mr. Lindley was the whole enterprise, especially in the building operations, as mentioned elsewhere. During the early years of his life he was the only Presbyterian clergyman in the part of the country where he labored. He died in his native State in 1857. He was a man of great personal courage, of more than average scholarship for his day and the conditions amid which he lived. He was also a man of unimpeachable integrity. Although not all the men appointed to a trusteeship of the O. U. took their appointments seriously while some did not accept their appointments at all, there was at least one exception, and that exception was Jacob Lindley. In the proceedings of the Supreme Court, it is recorded that Jacob Lindley was appointed a trustee of the O. U. in 1805; that he then resided in Athens and regularly performed his duty as a member of the board until 1828, in which year he removed to Cincinnati, having taken charge of a church in or near that city. But in 1829 he removed to the Flats of Grave Creek in Virginia, afterwards removing into Pennsylvania, and was a resident there on the eleventh of January, 1832. It also appeared from the record that one Thomas Bryce had been appointed to take the place of Mr. Lindley. The court, however, decided that "A legislative appointment of a successor without such resignation or adjudication confers no legal right upon the person appointed." At that time the trustees were appointed by the legislature.

As the Rev. Jacob Lindley seems to have been the most active man on the ground when the O. U. was getting under way, and as some of his descendants were in college long after his decease, it will be in order to follow his career to its end. The Lindley family first appears in New Jersey and later in Westmoreland County, Pennsylvania, in 1781, in which year the county was organized. The family was possessed of considerable means and took a leading part in the settlement of the southwestern corner of the Keystone State. Jacob Lindley was the seventh son of Demas Lindley and was born in 1774. He attended the Canonsburg Academy, where he was one of the founders of the Franklin Literary Society, Later, entering Princeton College, he was graduated from that institution in 1800. He was licensed to preach in 1803, removing to Waterford, O., shortly afterwards, where he was installed as the pastor of a church. A

[33]

little later he was appointed a trustee of the O. U. This position he held until his removal to the South in 1838 to visit one or more of his daughters. Not only the original building, but also the center building were erected under Mr. Lindley's auspices. He likewise was the leading spirit in the erection of the first Presbyterian church in Athens. It long stood on one of the corners in the center of the city on the site of the present church. Mr. Lindley married Hannah Dickey in 1800. One of his sons later became a missionary in Africa and two of his daughters married clergymen. One of his granddaughters became the wife of the Rev. C. W. Smith, afterwards a bishop in the M. E. Church. Jacob Lindley's sister Abigail married her cousin, Ziba Lindley, and their oldest daughter, Anna Lindley McVay, named her third son Jacob Lindley Mc-Vay, in honor of her uncle, Jacob Lindley McVay, who was born in 1818. This Jacob Lindley McVay was a familiar figure on the streets of Athens in the closing years of the nineteenth century up to the time of his death in 1901. It is a tradition among Mr. Lindley's descendants that the Center Building of the O. U., which is still in use although it is not the first building on the campus, was patterned after Nassau Hall. Desiring to know what light the records of the eastern institution would throw on this question, the compiler of this volume wrote to Mr. Leach, the reference librarian. That gentleman had the kindness to send the following data, which are slightly at variance with what has already been reported. "Jacob Lindley graduated from Princeton College in the class of 1800, and received his A. M. in 1805. He died in 1855. (?)

He was a trustee of the O. U. 1805-38, was president of the same from 1808 to 1838, professor of rhetoric and moral philosophy 1822-4, and professor of mathematics 1824-6." In 1829 Mr. Lindley returned to his native state, where he spent the remainder of his life in the family of Dr. Lutellus Lindley in Connellsville, his death occurring in 1857, when he was in the eighty-third year of his age. Mr. Leach continues, "I have consulted Mr. Collins, our secretary, who knows most about our alumni. He said that he had not known before of any connection between the architecture of your college and that of Princeton. The picture of your building, as given in Howe, is very interesting and suggests, after a fashion, Nassau Hall. There was published, however, a Dawkins print in 1764 which shows Nassau Hall with three entrances at the front and no towers at the end as now, since there was no need of an entrance at the end. (*The entrance at the west end of the Center Building is recent.*) This print was published as a frontispiece to an account of the college of New Jersey, issued by order of the trustees at Woodbridge, N. J., in 1764. This is a rare print and we have only one copy. There is a gable over the front entrance as today, while your building is plain across the front. The cupola on your building is much thinner and taller. I have no doubt, however, that since Lindley was a Princeton man, Nassau Hall influenced the planning of your building. It was only natural that a man should use his experience, and there were at that time not many buildings outside of Harvard, Yale, Columbia and a few others well enough known to influence college architecture." It may be confidently as-

[35]

serted that only one of the older college buildings
in this country was designed by a thoroughly
trained architect: that is "Old West" at Dickinson,
the plans for which were drawn by Major L'En-
fant, the designer of Washington City. It is about
143 feet in length, 46 in depth at the ends and a
few feet less at the center. It is four stories high
and built of limestone. The original building of
the O. U. was called the Academy and was completed in 1809. Its site is now marked by a pillar,
which already bears the stamp of vandalism. It
was a two-story brick structure and was probably
the first building erected northwest of the Ohio
River, for exclusively educational purposes. There
was but one room on each floor. After the erection
of the Center Building, it was leased to private
individuals and used as a school. It was torn down
in 1841. A two-story workshop was also erected a
short distance south of the main or Center Building in 1834. Its purpose was to provide "A system of Manual Labor for the employment of students." It is worth noting that about the same time
a like project was launched at Alleghany college,
at Lafayette, and perhaps at other places. Pre-
dictions that do not fail are difficult. At the present time to is easy to understand why such projects
were doomed to failure. There was little demand
for workshops in a country as new as was almost
the entire Union west of the Delaware River. In
the cut of the O. U. made from a photograph taken
about 1894 may be seen two small structures, one
of which was erected as a sort of miniature physical
laboratory, the larger one as a gymnasium. South
of the east wing, which is not visible in the cut,

almost an exact duplicate of the west wing, were also some small buildings mainly used as coal sheds. These have all long since been torn down and removed, as they ceased to be of use and were never ornamental.

Until near the close of the last century the students who roomed in the wings obtained their water for drinking from private wells outside the campus; then a drive well was put down not far from the southeast corner of the East Wing, by means of which potable water could be obtained. Rain water was collected in a cistern near the southeast corner of the center building and drawn up with a rope. Later some of this cistern water was used for laboratory purposes, being forced into a tank under the roof from which it descended by gravity. It is also a part of this story that not infrequently unsophisticated pedestrians who passed close to the wings were drenched with an artificial shower that had been collected in one of the upper rooms.

So far as the writer knows, the most numerously represented family among the graduates of the O. U. is that of W. W. McVay, a son of Jacob Lindley McVay and his wife, mentioned above, both of Athens County. "Lizzie" McVay soon after her graduation married a college mate, L. M. Gillilan, and removed to Salt Lake City, where she still resides. Mrs. Skinner (Gladys McVay) went off in the opposite direction and settled in Pittsburgh. For several years not a member of the younger generation lived in Athens County. At present, however, Herbert R. is county superintendent and Bertha is teaching in the home neighborhood. Anna Pearl, who was a member of the class of '92, after teaching for several years in her native State, entered Bryn Mawr College. For some time after graduation from that famous institution for women, she taught in Philadelphia, but later was called to New York, where for about a decade she has been Dean of Women in the Wadleigh High School and also teacher of Greek. The number of her pupils is about four thousand. A few years ago the trustees of the O. U. conferred upon her the honorary degree of L. H. D. This was not a gratuity; it was the deserved recognition of merit. Paul McVay Gillilan was a member of the class of 1915, and his wife, of the class of 1913. Martin Scott McVay, a son of H. R. mentioned above, following the example of his ancestor, Jacob Lindley, betook himself to Princeton and graduated with the class of '22, but almost five quarter centuries later. A daughter of H. R. McVay is now a Sophomore in the college. Thus the interrupted succession has been restored. "The king is dead. Long live the king."* It was no doubt due to the initial impulse given to higher education by the Presbyterians that there are so many titular colleges in southwestern Pennsylvania, and the conterminus territory. Of these there were about half a score, Alleghany being the farthest north. Although it is somewhat far afield, it was founded and maintained mainly by Presbyterians for nearly a score of years. The absurd, or at least peculiar, location of the State University of West Virginia within a few miles of the northern

* The Kirkendall family of Jackson County is represented by five brothers and sisters, and the Boyd-Lawrence clan by six members, not all graduates, however. To this clan belonged Margaret Boyd, after whom Boyd Hall on the college campus is named.

border of the State is due to the existence of an academy that antedated the university by a number of years. That the planting of colleges was sadly overdone soon became evident. However, we are not here concerned with the wisdom of the policy; we are concerned only with the fact. A former judge of the Ohio Supreme Court, who was for many years a resident of Athens where he died, and had a vivid recollection of pioneer days, was wont to say that although not a member of any church himself he attributed the comparatively peaceful conditions of the early day in Ohio and even in the regions farther west to the influence of the pioneer preachers. He placed the Methodists first. Most of these men were uneducated in the ordinary sense of the term, but they were not ignorant. Every one of them felt an irresistible call to the ministry and responded to the call with a zeal that no obstacles could dismay, no hindrances discourage, no dangers affright. They rode up and down the land preaching in private houses, in barns, in school-houses when there were any, and even in the open air. Francis Asbury came to America in 1771. His labors have left an enduring record in the history of our country. He has rightly been called "The Prophet of the long road." Up to the time of his death in 1816 he was almost constantly on the move. His devotion to his calling was equalled only by that of the early Jesuits. But how different was his influence! It is a question whether, as a general proposition, the present generation owes a great debt of gratitude to the "pioneers" who settled the Great West. Many of them, certainly a majority, came to better their condition, not that of their descendants. On the other hand, we epigoni owe much to the pioneer preachers. Most of them died as poor as they were born, because they did not work for themselves but for posterity. They sacrificed themselves for religion and morality, not to lay up treasure upon earth. (See also upon this subject the volume of Sweet mentioned elsewhere in this book. It is admirable for the light it throws upon the background of the O. U.) The Presbyterians, although they were early in the field, never gained a large following, while in higher education they soon fell far into the background. Their rigid organization and their formalism in modes of worship were probably somewhat of a drawback. Their motto was: "Let all things be done decently and in order." The Methodists were more concerned about what was done than how it was done. "The first census revealed that five per cent of the population in 1790 was distributed among several little islands almost lost in the wilderness. The first of these islands of population was in western Pennsylvania and contained about sixty-two thousand people. The second and third, containing in round numbers fifty-six thousand were clustered about Wheeling and the mouth of the Kanawha, while the fourth was in Kentucky and contained in round numbers seventy-four thousand souls."

Two events in the life of Mr. Lindley are of more than passing interest. Although not a practicing physician, he was endowed with an inquiring mind and the habits of thought of the investigator. There are good reasons for believing that he was the first person in the United States who made a practical

DR. THOMAS C. McCRACKEN
Dean of the College of Education

test of vaccination. In his boyhood an epidemic of smallpox had broken out in or near Connellsville, Pa., and the people were terror-stricken for the reason that they were utterly helpless, like everybody else in the world under similar circumstances. By some means young Lindley had learned, probably while at college, through French sources, that inoculation with cow-pox virus was a prophylactic against contagion. In later years, having procured some of the virus, he inoculated one of his children with it. As the child suffered no ill after-effects others were induced to try the remedy and the scourge was stayed. It is proper to remark, in this connection, that if the remedy had been used or suggested by a doctor of medicine instead of by a preacher it would have been regarded with more distrust or at least would have met with more opposition. It should be mentioned here that in 1798 Jenner published his "Inquiry into the Causes and Effects of Virulæ Vaccinæ." At this time young Lindley was a student at Princeton, while Philadelphia near by was the chief center of medical knowledge in the United States. Benjamin Rush, born in 1745, a graduate of the College of New Jersey and later of the University of Edinburg, was at that time a resident of the City of Brotherly Love, as were also other men of note in science and art, Ben Franklin being among them. It is also proper to remind the reader, in this connection, that Menasseh Cutler was a practicing physician. Until well along in the nineteenth century there were comparatively few educated men in this country except clergymen. Among lawyers and preachers were to be found some intelligent men, although they were not educated. But the country and small-town doctors were generally not only uneducated but ignorant and not unfrequently dissipated. The intimacy between Jacob Lindley and James Carnahan, later the ninth president of Princeton College, forms a charming episode in the life of both and is an interesting story. Although Carnahan was born in Carlisle, he was in some way attracted to southwestern Pennsylvania, where he made the acquaintance of young Lindley. It was agreed that both of them should attend college at Princeton. Although Dickinson was a Presbyterian institution until about 1833, a new building in process of erection at the end of the century was destroyed by fire. It is probable that this calamity turned young Carnahan's attention to the western college, but after consultation with Lindley, both decided that it would be to their interest to make the journey to the college of New Jersey. Young Lindley had a horse and some money; Carnahan had neither horse nor money except what he could borrow. It was accordingly agreed between the two young men that the horse could carry both of them and their belongings, but not at the same time. The two young men accordingly started from the Monongahela River, alternately riding the horse and walking. In this way they made the journey to their destination at the rate of thirty-five to forty miles a day. We are not here further concerned with James Carnahan; but we may mention that his career at Princeton was long and greatly to the advantage of the institution over which he presided.

VI

When the college campus was laid out a space on the north side was left vacant for a parade ground. It does not appear that it was ever used for this purpose; but it was left open and no trees were planted upon it, although the original forest had been removed. For many years it was occupied by the country people as a hitching-ground for their teams, and in the very nature of the case it was a veritable eye-sore, a sort of plague-spot to the æsthetic sense. In 1886 the trustees of the college brought a suit of ejectment against the village of Athens for the purpose of securing possession of this open space, mainly in order to abate a nuisance. The court of common pleas, however, held that the plaintiff had no valid claim to the property and the circuit court upheld the decision. It is probable that ten years subsequently the city council would have voluntarily renounced all claim to the disputed property. A few years later a "Monumental Association" was formed which was permitted to erect a soldiers' monument on the western half of the ground that had been in litigation. In 1896 the city council permitted the trustees of the college to occupy, or rather, to take possession of the eastern half, provided they kept it in due order and proper condition, at their own expense. This pledge has been faithfully observed to the present day.

Part of it was covered for a brief period during the World War by a building for soldiers. A short time after the close of the conflict not a trace of this "militarism" remained. Over the gateway at the northwest entrance to the campus and near the soldiers' monument are the two following inscriptions furnished by ex-president Eliot of Harvard:

"So enter that thou mayest daily grow in knowledge, wisdom and love.
So depart that thou daily mayest serve thy fellow men, thy country and thy God."

That the students of the college from its beginning almost unconsciously heeded this injunction and realized the necessity of self-improvement is demonstrated by the organization of literary societies. The Zelothian Society was organized in 1812. It seems, however, to have been a promise and a hope rather than a performance, probably owing to the paucity of students. This organization appears to have been preceded by the Polemic Society, although the records are not clear or at least incomplete. But in 1819 the Athenian Literary Society was organized by election of the usual officers. In 1836 this Society was incorporated with many rights and privileges. The first meeting of the Philomathean Society was held in 1822. In 1839 it was incorporated by an act of the legislature, at which time a constitution was adopted. These societies met every Friday evening in the strictest secrecy. For many years, so great was the desire to obtain members that incoming students were often met and pledges secured before they had entered the college building. It is a pity that no roster of students during the early years of the college exists, so far as is known. In the eighties an effort was made by the faculty to induce the societies to hold their meetings in the afternoons of Wednesday. This was done for a time, but was soon discontinued. The libraries of the societies, which for many years had occupied separate rooms, were eventually merged with that of the college. In the meantime, however, many books had been sold for a trifle because they had become a good deal shattered. Most of these books had only a sentimental value, but they ought not to have been disposed of.

In 1807 the Ohio legislature passed an act prohibiting lotteries on private account; but several times afterwards it authorized a lottery for a special purpose, among others one for the benefit of the O. U. This act was passed two days before the end of the year 1817. Why it was never put into effect is not known. It is reasonable to assume that the project originated with the board of trustees; that they made no use of it was probably due to negligence rather than to a disapproval of this method of raising money. When one examines the long list of laws passed by the legislature and the matters to which they relate, he is prompted to ask himself whether that body always took itself seriously and whether the board of trustees of the O. U. believed it to be in earnest. In 1827 a resolution was passed by the legislature requiring the trustees of the university to make an annual report to said body on the financial condition of the institution. No notice seems to have been taken of said resolution. At any rate in March, 1836, it was re-enacted at greater length, and again in January, 1837, reciting in the preamble that notwithstanding the previous resolutions they had remained uncomplied with. The constitution of 1851 contained two sections requiring annual reports to be made by the executive officers of all state institutions. Yet it does not appear that this requirement received any attention by the management of the O. U. The first report was made by president Scott for 1875-6. During the first half-century the existent vacancies were virtually filled by coöptation: that is, it was self-perpetuating. But with the adoption of the constitution just referred to, the appointing power passed into the hands of the Governor, where it still rests. As a matter of course, the personnel of the board changed very slowly, as there is no record of a removal for cause. There were, however, a few removals from the State. This automatically caused a vacancy, as only an elector can be a trustee. It may be said of the members what has often been said of postmasters: "few die and none resign." Several members served forty years, or at least held office for that length of time, and a few even longer. An unwise choice was now and then made, but on the whole it does not appear that the appointing power was, at any time, influenced by unworthy motives. As a matter of course, the two were always of the same political faith. Although such long-time appointments are entirely un-American, there are "knowing ones" who regard it as preferable to frequent changes. About twenty years previous to the Act of 1807 referred to above, the trustees of Dickinson College were granted authority to raise money by means of a lottery. As the times were unpropitious, the project amounted to little, as the sum realized was only about two thousand dollars. However, for some time afterward the legislature of that State distributed money among its colleges. These donatives seem to have ceased when most of the institutions passed under denominational control. It is probable that the trustees of the O. U. made no effort to put this permission into effect, owing to the extreme scarcity of money.

It is worth noting that the growth of public sentiment against lotteries in this country was slower than in England, where they were made illegal by the Gambling Act of 1802. In the United States, lotteries and all games of chance were not entirely forbidden by law until the beginning of the present century. A curious fact in comparative morality is revealed by the existence of lotteries in most countries of continental Europe, where they are still in vogue for all sorts of objects, both sacred and secular. We have here one of the forms of restricting personal liberty that is peculiar to the Anglo-Saxon people. It is hard to prove that there is anything intrinsically immoral in lotteries or in games of chance. When a man buys a lottery ticket authorized by his government, he is reasonably certain that if he loses, his money will at least aid some worthy object. Albeit, the American public is constantly invited to invest in enterprises that are deliberate frauds, or nearly so. In most cases only the promoters realize anything. So strong is the proclivity of people for taking chances that notwithstanding the most stringent prohibitory laws, our public continues to allow itself to be wheedled out of large sums, apparently and chiefly for the reason that it will persist in taking chances. A factor that doubtless had a retarding influence on the growth of the O. U., numerically at least, and its standing with the legislature was the rise of denominational colleges. It had no organized clientele; on the other hand, the clergy of the denominational institutions were recruiting agents for them and devoted to their interest. One trustee of the O. U. and a prominent alumnus known to the writer was at least mildly hostile to the institution he had been appointed to serve. When the president discovered his inconsistent attitude he suggested to the gentleman the propriety of sending his resignation to the Governor. As the number of prospective students, until some time after the close of our sectional war, was limited, it is probably true, as a general statement, that every student who entered a college meant one less for some other. The management of some colleges, or at least their presidents, were outspokenly hostile to the institution at Athens, both before the public and the legislature. After the establishment of the university at Columbus, its management did not look with favor on its older sisters at Athens and Oxford. As we approach the end of the nineteenth century conditions began to change, or at least public opinion began to undergo an evolutionary process. Experience has demonstrated that an increase of the number of students in one institution does not necessarily mean a decrease at another. Besides, going to college is to most young people like going to the seashore: the sea is about equally salty everywhere. Recently a condition of affairs has supervened which made it necessary for college faculties to discourage and even to restrict attendance rather than to encourage it. Between 1830 and 1841 the following institutions were chartered: Kenyon, Denison, Marietta, and the Ohio Wesleyan. There were probably others in the State that continue to function in a small way, but more that have "gone under." Marietta College had been preceded, for some years, by a Teachers' Seminary, with which, however, it had no organic connection. By 1840 the attendance had risen to fifty-three, of which number fifteen were Virginians. At a time when commerce and travel overland was slow and costly and when during at least eight months of the year it was comparatively cheap by water, an institution on or near a navigable stream like the Ohio naturally drew the attention of the Virginians living along rivers flowing into the Ohio more to the west than to the east. It is astonishing how rapidly steamboats were built after their success had been demonstrated. They are reported to have appeared in New Orleans almost as soon as Louisiana was admitted into the Union. It was said, probably with some exaggeration, that they were sometimes built to run on a heavy dew.

In the instructive volume by Charles Ambler entitled: "Sectionalism in Virginia," we find the record of this tendency. We read that "out of a total enrolment of 112 residents of the University of Virginia only twelve came from the counties west of the Blue Ridge." By 1846 the total enrolment from Virginia had increased to 134, but the number from west of the Blue Ridge had increased by only two. In 1839 there were twice as many residents from western Virginia attending colleges in Ohio and Pennsylvania as were enrolled in the institution in eastern Virginia. The number attending Marietta alone was fifteen. If the foregoing figures are correct there must have been a relatively rapid increase at Marietta at this time. Albeit, the actual figures are of little importance, the chief interest is in the westward tendency they indicate. Although the attendance of many of the students was very irregular and there was a good deal of "doubling up," it is a question whether any valid objection can be raised against this procedure, although it is now almost everywhere discarded. Young men were permitted to advance as fast as they could, without being limited to a certain number of recitation hours per week. It is assumed that a student who gets his lessons easily will spend his spare time wisely. In most cases it is an unjustified assumption. By the current method the obtainment of an education is made a matter of drill, students like soldiers being required to march in lock-step. Results were considered more than the methods by which they were obtained. A former governor of Ohio, a major-general in the army, a cabinet officer, a member of Congress and the occupant of other civil offices did two years of college work in one. It is the experience of all teachers that some students can do twice as much work in the same time as others and do it as well if not better, except in the laboratory. When the writer was in college it was impossible for a student to take more than about sixteen class-room hours work per week; there were three recitations per day for five days and one on Saturday morning. During two terms there were afternoon lectures, but they required little preparation. All the students were obliged to be present at the Saturday morning exercises, but only a few performed.

VII

In 1822 a faculty was organized with Rev. James Irvine as president and professor of mathematics. Mr. Lindley was also made a member of the teaching personnel. Mr. Irvine was born in Washington County, N. Y., and graduated from Union College, now Union University, in 1821. He was at once elected president and professor as stated above. A few months after his election he was obliged to apply for leave of absence and for some reason not now known he never returned to Athens. He resigned a short time subsequently and after a brief residence in New York city accepted the pastorate of a Presbyterian church at West Hebron in his native county, but died not long after. Robert G. Wilson was born in Lincoln County, N. C., in 1768. He received his baccalaureate degree at Dickinson College with the class of 1790. Two years later he was licensed to preach by the Presbytery of his native State, in which he also occupied pulpits until 1805. Thereafter, for about nineteen years, he was the pastor of a Presbyterian church in Chillicothe which was at that time the capital of the State. When it was first organized the number of counties was only about half a score, nearly all of them lying along the Ohio River. Much of the northwestern portion was still unorganized. Mr. Wilson must have attracted a good deal of attention far from the scene of his labors, as Princeton gave him the honorary degree of D. D. in 1818. He was chosen a trustee of the O. U. in 1809 and president

in 1824. He held the presidency for fourteen years, when he resigned on account of advancing age, although he lived until 1851. President Wilson was succeeded by William H. McGuffey, whose name is familiar to almost every American who attended a public school in the last half of the nineteenth century. He was born in Washington County, Pa., in 1806, but when the son was quite young his father moved into Ohio, where the lad grew to manhood. The elder McGuffey, who was a sturdy farmer, saw little use for what is called education and discouraged his son's fondness for books. As there were at that time no schools in the region where the family lived, the boy walked several miles two or three times a week to recite to a preacher the lessons he had learned at night by the light of a torch made of burning pine-knots. When the youth was eighteen years old his teacher considered him sufficiently advanced to enter Washington College, an institution that had been chartered in 1806, and which we shall meet again in the course of this narrative. Young McGuffey received his baccalaureate degree in 1826, having earned his way by teaching from time to time wherever he could find employment. His last engagement of this kind was at Paris, Ky., where he taught a school in a smoke-house that was still standing a few years ago. In 1836 a college was organized in Cincinnati and McGuffey was elected president. But after an existence of three years it went the way of many similar and more or less ambitious enterprises that were launched in those years all over this country. After his rather brief but stormy experience at Athens, McGuffey returned to Cincinnati in 1843 to accept

[52]

a position in the Woodward High School. Some
years later William Rives, a member of the Board
of Visitors of the University of Virginia, heard Dr.
McGuffey lecture and was so much impressed with
the personality of the man and his power as a
speaker that upon his recommendation the clergyman was invited to become a member of the faculty
of the southern institution. In its service he spent
the remainder of his life, teaching, preaching and
lecturing. One day in the spring of 1873, after de-
livering a lecture to children, he was taken ill with
an affection of the brain and died a few weeks later.
During his residence in Cincinnati he was one of a
coterie of schoolmen who became dissatisfied with
the textbooks then in use. They acocrdingly decided to prepare a series on a rational plan. The
series afterwards called the "Eclectie" was the result, although it was gradually much changed.
The Readers were assigned to McGuffey, as he was
thought to be the best qualified member for the task.
They contained no original contributions by him,
but included a few by E. D. Mansfield, who was
one of the junta. Dr. McGuffey was a fluent
speaker but not a profound thinker. His manner
in the pulpit and on the platform was expository
rather than hortatory. He was better fitted for
teaching than for preaching. He does not seem to
have written anything that has been preserved. A
citizen of Athens was wont to relate that in his
boyhood he frequently drove president McGuffey
to churches and schoolhouses where he was to
preach. On such occasions he sometimes requested
the youth to suggest some verse of Scripture to be
used as a text for the sermon. Although ordained

as a regular minister in the Presbyterian church, it
does not appear that he ever held a regular pastorate. His remains, together with those of two
members of his family, lie buried in a cemetery at
University, Va. During the past few years two or
more McGuffey Societies have been formed and the
lot in the cemetery has been put in fair condition.
What a fine advertisement, in the best sense of the
word, it would have for the modern Athenians, if
they had kept Dr. McGuffey to the end of his days.
He was one of the prophets who was without honor
among his kindred and his countrymen. Perhaps
under similar conditions he would not have fared
better elsewhere. Owing to the failure of the trustees to obtain a reappraisement of the college lands,
they found themselves unable to pay a debt of about
fourteen thousand dollars that had been accumulated by 1844. After the resignation of President
McGuffey, the college seems to have been carried on
in a haphazard sort of way until April 2, 1844, when
it was resolved that "in view of the present condition
of the university and in consequence of its financial
embarrassments and the falling off in the attendance of the students, it appears indispensable, for
a time, to suspend the ordinary operations of the
college." During the suspension, which was to begin on the first Thursday in August, 1845, and to
continue for three years unless "circumstances jus-
tify an earlier resumption," the Rev. Aaron Williams was authorized to continue the work of the
academy or preparatory department, at a salary of
six hundred dollars per annum, with the addition
of tuition fees until the whole should amount to
eight hundred dollars. Mr. Williams was also to

have general charge and oversight of the property. For two years he was the entire teaching force; during the third year he had an assistant. In November, 1847, the trustees decided to reorganize, in accordance with the resolution of 1845, and to resume operations the next fall. Work was accordingly taken up again with a very small number of students. No catalog can be found, after the resumption of earlier date than 1850. In the list of the faculty appears the name of the Rev. Aaron Williams as professor of Greek and Latin. The number of students was about one hundred. Of these, sixteen were in the higher classes, the Freshmen numbering five. It may be remarked here that all the writer's efforts to obtain information about the aforementioned Mr. Williams were futile. He was reported to have gone South and one of his sons—whether he had more than one is not known —"turned up" in Washington about the close of our sectional war. Several years ago a son was reported to be in business in Memphis, Tenn., but a letter of inquiry addressed to mayor of that city remained unanswered. Here and there was found the trail of ardent spirits, which, be it noted, was also discovered now and then in the earlier history of the O. U. A man can whitewash his dark deeds while he lives by applying a fresh coat as often as he thinks it necessary, but the time will come when he cannot do the work himself, nor hire anyone else to do it for him.

Alfred Ryors was born in Philadelphia in 1812. Left an orphan at an early age, he was placed in the family of Rev. Robert Steele at Abingdon, a place that cannot now be found on any map, by whom he was prepared for college. He entered the Freshman class at Jefferson College, where he remained two years. Then he taught Greek and Latin for a short time in a private school, but returned to college and graduated with the class of 1834. He taught for a brief period in the preparatory department of Lafayette College, which had been chartered in 1832. In 1838 he was elected professor of mathematics in the O. U. About the same time he was licensed to preach by the presbytery of Philadelphia and shortly afterwards married the daughter of Judge Walker of Athens, Ohio. When the O. U. was closed owing to the adverse legislation of 1843, he was called to the professorship of mathematics in the State University at Bloomington, Ind., where he remained until elected to the presidency of the O. U. In 1852 he was recalled to the Indiana University, but resigned at the end of the year, a crisis having overtaken the institution similar to that which closed the O. U. For a short period he occupied the pulpit of a church in his adopted State, when he was elected professor of mathematics in Center College, Ky. He subsequently became its president, in which position he died in 1852. As a mathematician his rank among his peers was high.

For two or three decades after the opening of the O. U. the authorities seem to have issued no catalogue. The college library contains a fragmentary pamphlet on which some one has written the date "1832." This is part of a catalogue, although the date is somewhat problematical. But it cannot be far astray, as Dr. Wilson was president, and he retired in 1838. At this time the num-

LINDLEY HALL
Outside the campus

ber of professors was four, including the president, and there was an "Academical Preceptor." There were forty-seven students in the collegiate and twenty-five in the academical department. Among the Seniors were six from Marietta but only two in the lower classes. Ten of the students were from Virginia and three from other southern States. As Marietta College was opened about this time, few students after that event came to Athens. It may be mentioned in this connection that W. D. Emerson was a member of the class of 1833 (see post VII*b*). Tuition in the college classes was twenty dollars a year and students were allowed to occupy unfurnished rooms in the college, if they desired. As the Wings had not yet been erected and as all the college activities were carried on in the center building, it must have been rather densely populated. The price of boarding, washing included, was from one dollar to one dollar and a half per week. The reader is also informed that in addition to the studies enumerated, the afternoon of every Wednesday is devoted to exercises in declamation and the writing of compositions. "Each student delivers an oration and exhibits a composition once in two weeks." In the catalogue for 1851 the Seniors number two, the Juniors five, the Sophomores and Freshmen ten each. The preparatory students number thirty-seven. The increase of students after the resumption seems to have been fairly rapid. The next year there were about a hundred in attendance, although there were only sixteen in the higher classes, the Freshmen numbering no more than five.

The oldest catalogue that has been preserved is that of 1843. At that time the faculty consisted of five men, William H. McGuffey being the president. There was a professor of Greek and one of Latin. The number of students was one hundred and eleven, of whom sixty were in the collegiate department. In said catalogue we may read that "the student, at the commencement of the Junior year may elect to continue the mathematics course or to commence the study of French in the place thereof." In the catalogue for 1860-1 appears for the first time the name of a professor of French and German. There were, at the time, two literary societies, as has been mentioned elsewhere in this volume, and a Natural History Society. Evidently not all instruction was derived from textbooks. "The necessary expenses of an academic year, exclusive of furniture, books and clothes will be from $85 to $105, in other words about one hundred dollars per annum." It has just been mentioned that in 1850-1 the number of students was sixty-four, of which number a few more than one-half were classed as preparatory and irregular. Numerically the status of the university was quite as low many years later, as has been shown elsewere in this volume. The conditions for admittance were, at least on paper, comparatively high. The postulant must be acquainted with Greek and Latin grammar, Latin reader, Virgil's "Aeneid," Cicero's "Orations," and the Greek Reader. Latin is continued through two-thirds of the Junior year and Greek 'one term longer, there being three terms in the year.

Solomon Howard was born near Cincinnati in 1811. He did the work of his Freshman and Sophomore years at Miami University, and that of the two following years at Augusta College, where he

received his degree. This college was one of the
tangible evidences of the rising enthusiasm for
higher education in the Methodist denomination.*

* In the course of my researches I came across the trail of
this somewhat elusive college several times; but all my efforts
to follow it to its source were fruitless, until my attention was
drawn to a volume entitled: "Circuit Rider Days along the Ohio,"
by W. W. Sweet, in which I found all the information necessary
for my purpose. Augusta College was founded in 1822 by the
joint action of the Kentucky and Ohio Conferences of the Methodist Episcopal Church. This was also an important year in the
history of the O. U., as may be read in another part of this
volume. The site was chosen for the reason that its situation
on the banks of the Ohio River made it comparatively easy of
access in the "early days." The location of the town is about
midway between Portsmouth and Cincinnati. However, after an
existence of a century posterior to the date above given it had
hardly reached a population of a thousand souls. In 1825 a
three-story building was erected and the college set in motion.
The Rev. J. B. Finley was its first president. After his death the
Rev. Martin Ruter was placed in charge. John P. Durbin was
made professor of languages. He was born in Bourbon County,
Ky., in 1800 and was for some time a student at Miami University. He was president of Dickinson College 1833-45, and for
more than twenty years Missionary Secretary of the Methodist
Episcopal Church. Martin Ruter, who was a native of Massachusetts, was one of the first men in American Methodism to
receive the degree of D. D. He was president of Alleghany College for some years, but died in Texas in 1838. In the same
year J. P. Tomlinson, who was president of the college, delivered an address on a liberal education which was printed in the
town. It was a creditable performance both for the author and
the printer. For a number of years Augusta College was mod-
erately successful; then it was removed to Lexington in the same
State, where its subsequent career was brief. Probably the
cause might be summed up in three words: "Too far south."
The college, however, gave to the church such men as Bishop
Foster, professor John Miley and professor W. G. Williams, long
connected with the Ohio Wesleyan University. Randolph S. Foster was born in Clermont County, O., in 1820. The only systematic education he received he obtained in Augusta, which he
left at seventeen years of age to enter the ministry. He was
for some time president of the Northwestern University and later
of Drew Theological Seminary. He was elected bishop in 1872.
In a recent article on the early history of Kentucky we read
that "the great prehistoric cemetery underlying Augusta was an
almost solid layer of skeletons. Some of these are of men who
must have been seven or eight feet tall."

A PIONEER COLLEGE

Not long after his graduation young Howard went to Missouri, where he assisted in organizing a college, but soon returned to Ohio and entered the ministry. Among his stopping-places was the home of Jesse Grant, father of General Grant, later President of the United States. Subsequently he was one of the three professors who opened the O. W. U. at Delaware, in November, 1844. Soon after he was elected president of a female college at Springfield, O., and president of the O. U. in 1852. Twenty years later he died in California, whither he had gone in quest of health.

President Howard's manner in the pulpit was somewhat lacking in grace, and his language sometimes more forceful than elegant. But his evident sincerity won for him the respect of even those whose practices he denounced. Dr. Howard was the first Methodist elected president of the O. U. Although the preponderance of the Presbyterians continued for some time longer at Miami, it had been gradually waning both in Pennsylvania and in Ohio. Mention has already been made of the fact that two Presbyterian colleges in the former State came under the control of the Methodists early in the thirties. The transfer was not a case of displacement but of replacement—the most feasible plan for getting rid of an intolerable burden. It was a sort of Solonian *Seisachtheia* modernized.

Our sectional war had a disturbing influence upon the affairs of the college during the presidency of Dr. Howard as it had upon every other college in the country. The salaries of the president and professors were $1200 and $900, respectively. But this was a slight increase over the years immediately preceding and a considerable increase over former years. It does not appear that they were more than $2500 and $1500 at any time during the nineteenth century. It is probable that the purchasing power of money was at least three times as great as it was before the construction of railroads made the transportation of commodities easy and comparatively cheap. The mere statement of this fact, however, conveys but little information. The important fact to be considered is that the wants of the average American are at least ten times as great as they were less than a century ago. Although high thinking is not an inseparable concomitant of plain living, we may take for granted that the former was at least as high as it is now, whatever is or may have been the mode of life. The twentieth century has engendered few new ideas, although it has been fraught with many new discoveries and inventions. The fundamental principles of education are at least as old as the days of Plato and Aristotle. Educators are still engaged in devising methods for putting those principles into practice. Although the salaries of all teachers are much higher now than they were even two or three decades ago, there is a far greater clamor about their insufficiency than ever.

William H. Scott was born near Athens, O., in 1840. He received his A. B. at the O. U. with the class of 1862. After teaching for some time in the public schools of Athens, he was elected principal of the preparatory department of his *alma mater,* at which time he was also admitted toes the ministry of the M. E. Church. After serving two pastorates he was elected professor of Greek and from 1872 to 1883 he was president of the O. U., being at the same time also professor of philosophy. From the latter date until 1895 he held a similar position in the State University at Columbus. Thereafter until 1910 he was professor of philosophy in the same institution, at which time he retired from active work. One of his sons (Charles Felton), who entered upon his college career at Athens, has been professor of electrical engineering in the Sheffield (Yale) Scientific School since 1911. Ex-president Scott's educational activities have been wholly confined to his native State. He delivered many lectures and addresses and in his later years made some noteworthy contributions to philosophical journals. It was during his presidency that an act was passed by the legislature which considerably increased the revenues of the college, but also led to a long and bitterly contested lawsuit.

The names of only two colored men appear on the alumni roll of the O. U. Of these, John Newton Templeton was a clergyman and teacher for some time; but nothing is known of his later life nor of the place and date of his death. The career of John C. Corbin, who received his degree in 1853, was altogether creditable. He was the editor of several different newspapers. For one term he was State Superintendent of Public Instruction of Arkansas and also president of the State Colored Teachers Association. He is said to have been an accomplished linguist and a musician of considerable ability. The date of his death is not known to the writer. At various times during the last half century a few colored students have been in attendance, but for a short time only. There is no apparent objection to their presence on the part of either teachers or taught. At different times at least three colored men were members of the board. One of them is said to have been a graduate of Dartmouth College; at any rate he was fully qualified for the position both by education and character. Another was reported to be totally unfit, for reasons that are not known to the writer. His term of service was comparatively short. The third member could hardly be taken seriously, though he seems to have been a man of good character. The name of the first alumna appears with the class of 1873. The name of another young woman appears with the class of 1876 and the names of two may be found with the class of 1879, after which date the names of women are of frequent occurrence.

In the list of the faculty for 1883-4 the name of
Charles W. Super appears as president *pro tem,*
and in that of the next year as president. There
was an interregnum of some months, during which
period the trustees were seeking a successor to president Scott; but the quest proved fruitless. The
outlook was too gloomy. The final choice was probably determined by the faculty; at any rate, it was
reported to be entirely satisfactory to the little company. They may have thought that although in
Cowtown the goat is not big, in Catville he is a
giant. The most discouraging phase of the situation was that nearly all the trustees had given up
hope for the "old college." They believed that as
it had never received an appropriation for current
expenses the legislature could not be persuaded to
break a precedent under existing conditions. After
the president-elect had succeeded in making an appointment with the finance committee of the Senate
—the appropriation bill had already passed the
House without allowing anything for the O. U.—
but one of the trustees thought it worth while to attend the hearing; and he lived in a distant part of
the State. Albeit, the hearing produced results.
The following data appear in the catalogues for this
period. In 1880 the graduating class numbered 4.
1882 it consisted of five members, while in the next
two years the numbers were four and two, respectively. In 1867 there were only two graduates. But
in 1891-2-3 and 5 the graduating classes numbered
11, 18, 20 and 15, respectively. Before this time the

largest outgoing classes had been 13 in 1831 and
in 1870. The entire number of names in the catalogue for '95 is 310. The faculty for the same year
was composed of 28 persons. It should, however,
be kept in mind by the reader that not all students
who are classed as Seniors in any year received degrees in the same year, while a few received two
degrees. Besides, from the very nature of the case,
when students are irregular in their attendance, an
accurate classification is impossible. While, therefore, the names of the students represent an exact
total, their division into classes is not altogether
trustworthy. The catalogue for 1900-1 contains the
names of 440 students. For many years the graduates had not all been of the same rank, some receiving the degree of A. B., others that of B. S.,
the latter degree representing about one year's less
work. This difference seems to have been abolished
under the regime of president Scott. The only
fairly uniform standard for graduation was the degree of A. B.; but as has just been pointed out, the
O. U., like most degree-conferring institutions, at
least in the West, while granting two degrees on the
same occasion, did not claim that they were equiva-
lent, although it is probable that the recipients made
such a claim, while the general public was in no position to discriinate. It does not appear that two
degrees were granted in the colleges east of the Ohio
river. Albeit, no expert would assert that the
same degree even at the same institution always rep-
resents the same value.

For various reasons the years immediately following the departure of president Scott were tempestuous and often strenuous for his successor. Ow-

ing to the straitened condition of the finances, he
was almost compelled to spend nearly or quite as
much time in the classroom as the other members of
the teaching force. He was general overseer of the
buildings and grounds because there was no one else
upon whom the responsibility could be placed. He
was expected to deal with all cases of discipline that
were not of a sufficiently serious nature to require
faculty action. He was to a large extent the financial agent whose special duty it was to make sure
that one hundred cents in value were realized upon
every dollar expended, besides being perpetual
lobbyist, as the legislature met every year and the
lobbying could not all be done at Columbus. "Them
times" the problem of discipline was a more serious
one than with a much larger number of students in
subsequent years. The undergraduates were a good
deal given to "kicking," even if, unlike Jeshurun,
they had not waxed fat. The president could not
consider himself included in the promise to the children of Israel that he should be the head and not
the tail, or that he should be above only and not
beneath. He was expected to be everywhere and
was assumed to be responsible for everything that
was what it should not. The latent hostility to the
college on the part of some of the lessees, which had
not diminished but rather intensified by adverse
court decisions, sometimes found active expression
in vandalism by hooligans in town; and it would be
rash to affirm that they were never aided or at least
abetted by some of the students. When one looks
back upon those "parlous" days they appear rather
ridiculous; but they were often serious enough and
more than enough for those immediately concerned.

[66]

If the president's position was a bed of roses, as some persons of limited experience fatuously supposed it to be, it was one in which the thorns largely predominated and from which the soporifics were wholly absent. It is possible that his drooping spirits were sometimes buoyed up by the thought to which Jonah is said to have given utterance when he bade farewell to the big fish that had been his unsought lodging-place for three days: "You can't keep a good man down." For a number of years the president was compelled to serve himself as secretary. A writing machine cost money and an expert to manipulate it cost more, and where was the necessary cash to come from? Hence the president was obliged to do his writing in the way Sairy Gamp raised the orphan—by hand. It is probable that his correspondents regarded this as the "most unkindest cut" of all. It should however be said, in this connection, that it has not yet been determined which of the presidents of the O. U. during the first century of its existence wrote the most execrable hand. In those days systematic athletics were hardly known and many of the students felt impelled to work off their superfluous energies in ways that were dark and tricks that were sometimes nasty. Eventually they erected a fairly large building about fifty feet south of Cutler Hall, mainly at their own expense. They also provided considerable apparatus. But as there was no systematic oversight one piece after another was broken and not replaced. The iconoclasts seemed not to realize that only a bad bird befouls its own nest. These activities doubtless differ a good deal in different institutions and even at the same institutions at

[67]

different periods. There has also been, during recent years, considerable abatement of the friction
between faculty and students all over the country.
The time is not far distant when the latter considered the former a sort of necessary evil that had to
be endured for the sake of certain benefits, real or
imaginary, which they could confer and which could
be obtained in no other way. Speaking generally,
most students were wont to regard the faculty as a
body of oppressors who were always ready to coöperate in harassing their more or less helpless victims,
and whose chief joy it was to take all joy out of
life or at least out of the life of young people. To
many it seems never to occur that when an instructor insists on maintaining a high standard of scholarship in his department it is quite as much to the
interest of the student to respond to the demand
as it is to the instructor who makes the demand.
In after years a student does not often speak kindly
of a teacher who was "easy." On the other hand,
it would probably be impossible, at any rate it
would not be a small matter, to find a faculty con-
sisting of even a dozen members, in which there are
no intriguers and schemers for their own interest
against their peers. Some see their own merits by
introspection only and the demerits of their colleagues by observation. To a certain class of ob-
servers the former do not exist at all while the
latter exist in large quantities. Moreover, there
are doubtless few colleges among whose trustees
there are no members who are without deserving
friends to be taken care of or deserving kinsfolk to
provide for after the manner of winners in a political contest. Being unable to rise on their merits

[68]

they are obliged to win on their influence. Presidents of colleges and even governors of States have been known to reward their friends who wanted to get in and to punish their enemies who had to be ejected if they proved refractory. A rainbow is a beautiful object only when seen from a distance; a nearer view dispels the illusion. An illusion that is dispelled by proximity is that a board of college trustees or a board of education is always composed of men of high character and unselfish aims. Such men may be found in every board; but they are not always, perhaps not generally, in the majority. After a man has been a student in a college and in a university, a member of two or three different faculties, a president and a member of a board of trustees, he has not necessarily been in hell, but he is almost certain to have been in purgatory. If, after all these experiences, he still survives, he is surely fit for heaven.

In the eighties we decided to equip the rooms in the two wings with the heavier articles of furniture in order to lighten the expenses of the occupants and incidentally to make a little money for the college. At that time there were no establishments in Athens for the sale of second-hand furniture. The most important item was the bedstead; and in order to get something that was durable we bought about a dozen made of iron. Alas, we soon found that the occupants of the rooms regarded these bedsteads as a challenge to their iconoclastic proclivities and they made themselves ready to meet it. Although they could not be broken, they could be twisted out of shape and made useless. It could not be said of them, it is true, as was said of the well-known Kilkenny cats: "There weren't any," though there might as well not have been since they were worthless. We could not hold the occupants of the rooms responsible for the damage, as they could solemnly affirm that they were innocent. Although the Diabolonians did not break or damage their own furniture, they invaded the premises of their neighbors and thus provoked reprisals. Even the doors were not proof against house-breaking. It was often both comical no less than exasperating to behold the expression of injured innocence on the face of a student when challenged with damaging the furniture of his room. It may be stated as a general fact that although college students will rarely tell a deliberate lie, the truth is sometimes so mangled and tangled up with falsehood and understatement that they cannot be separated. It has been said of this class of human beings that although some of them often fail to keep all of the ten commandments, there is one, the eleventh, that none of them ever fail to keep: "Thou shalt not get found out." Notwithstanding their numerous sins of omission and commission, American college students are an important and increasingly influential portion of the American people, in spite of the fact that now and then one of their number needs not only to be educated but also to be civilized. About the same time we also equipped the basement of the east wing with a culinary department and provided a cook. This arrangement was not a permanent success, owing to the conduct of certain "lewd fellows of the baser sort." Perhaps the cook did not assert her authority with sufficient vigor. At any rate, there were usually a few boys who were unconscious imitators of the animal that is an abomination to the Jews; for while they did not put their feet in the trough, there being no trough, they did other things that were hardly less out of place and equally offensive to good manners. There are other animals besides quadrupeds and feathered bipeds that have some habits which are certainly not nice. In a few years the club arrangement was abandoned. Later, boarding clubs were organized in private houses and the boarders who would not or could not "conduct themselves decently and in order" were invited to seek more congenial company. It may also be mentioned, in this connection, that "de worl do move," *tempora mutantur,* etc. A quarter of a century earlier when the price of table-board began to rise, owing to the sectional war, a dozen students at Dickinson college set up or fitted out a culinary department at their own expense in the basement of "Old West." Soon a second club was formed, then a third and perhaps a fourth, each club regulating its "grub" according to the financial means of its members or their liberality. There never was any trouble with "hooligans and hellicans." Besides, hardly anybody would be stupid enough to try to pull down an edifice that he had assisted in building. It must, however, be admitted that the mental operations of students of either sex are not to be explained by the ordinary laws of human conduct. Sometimes his ways (and hers, too) are past finding out— until afterwards. In days gone by we heard or read, now and then, of a student who injured his health by a too close application to his books; but for many years no case has been reported. The "overworked teacher" has also disappeared from the land, or at least from the printed page.

No wise frog objects to being reminded now and then that he was once a tadpole.

[71]

VII*b*

At the end of 1923 there were about one hundred and fifty colleges and universities having an endowment of a million dollars or more. Of these at least a dozen reported ten million dollars and over in invested funds. Of the entire number about a dozen are in Ohio and as many in Pennsylvania. Absolute accuracy is unattainable for reasons that will readily occur to the reader. Besides, these figures do not include more than one-fourth of the colleges and titular universities in the country and other endowed educational agencies. It is interesting and instructive to recall that this large sum was donated during the last fifty years. Half a century ago the number of colleges in the country—there were no universities except on paper—with a million-dollar endowment was a rarity, if any such existed. A few interesting and instructive inferences may be drawn from these facts and figures. It is not probable that there will be a diminution of donations for many years to come. The South and parts of the West have only quite recently made a beginning. On the other hand, the income from invested funds will ere long begin to decrease as the opportunities for profitable investments must necessarily soon become fewer. Another is that the chief burden or responsibility for providing the means of higher education will fall more and more on the endowed institutions, as there is no limit to private beneficence, and therefore no limit to the potential resources of such institutions. This cannot be affirmed of tax-supported institutions. In this direc-

CUTLER HALL

From the northwest.   Remodeled.

tion the limit will probably soon be reached and
further development will be difficult. These institutions will therefore be compelled to restrict their
activities to the subjects in which the public is
mainly interested, and which it considers of practical value, leaving the cultural subjects to the endowed institutions. It would be hard to persuade
a legislature to appropriate money for the equipment of an exploring expedition to some part of
the world that has only an antiquarian interest, or
for researches that may end in failure. On this
point the figures given out by the Presbyterian
Church have just come to hand. They are instructive, interesting and typical for all the churches in
the Union. Ten years ago the productive endowments of the colleges of said body were somewhat
over thirteen million dollars. In 1923 they had
risen to nearly double this sum. The total assets
on the colleges was over thirty-two million dollars.
By 1923 they had increased to nearly fifty-eight
million dollars. The annual current expenses had
grown from two and a half million dollars to nearly
six million dollars. In the matter of personal giving the United Presbyterians rank highest, being
nearly thirty-six dollars per individual.

While there is little doubt that the early land-
grant colleges were for the most part sadly mismanaged and that the prospective beneficiaries received
much less than their due, there is a good deal of
palliation for what seems to have been bad management. Land was enormously plenty and prices
low. On the other hand, most of the sales made
under the Morrill act, while perhaps legally straight
were morally crooked. Like almost everything

[73]

done by the federal government between 1860 and
'76 the land-grant business was permeated with
graft, fraud and peculation. Much of the loss was
probably made good by later taxpayers for the
simple reason that there was no other way out of
the impasse. Almost to the end of the nineteenth
century the O. U. received no private donations.
Then W. D. Emerson of the class of '33, who was
at the time a resident of Marietta, bequeathed to
the institution one thousand dollars, the interest of
which was to be awarded every second year to the
student or graduate of the college who should write
the best original poem. Mr. Emerson's own contributions to the poetical literature of his native state
consist of a volume of verse entitled: "Rhymes of
Culture, Movement and Repose," published in Cincinnati in 1874. The author informs the reader that
"The following metrical essays are respectfully offered to the public, being a selection from a variety
of articles with the composition of which the author
has amused some of his leisure hours during nearly
forty years of diversified labor and study." The
longest poem is entitled "The Corn Field." It con-
sists of 140 Spencerian stanzas and constitutes a
sort of rustic drama or epic. The volume, while on
the whole containing little good poetry, is not lacking in some verse which now and then gives the
reader a glimpse of the life of the pioneers that is
both pleasing and instructive. This is particularly
true of "The Corn Field."

Here is our author's tribute to

AND ITS BACKGROUND

ATHENS, OHIO.

Sweet Athens! the home of learning and beauty,
  How I long for thy hills and thy rich, balmy air!
For thy wide-spreading green, smiling sweetly on duty,
  And the valley beneath and the stream winding
      there!
On the north the high rock, on the south the lone
      ferry;
  The mill on the east, and the mill on the west;
The lawn, where the gravest at play-hours were merry,
  And the walks by the footsteps of beauty made blest.

The old college building, where Enfield and Stewart
  Oft found me ensconced in the cupola cool,
While I glanced now and then, 'mid the study of true
     art,
  At the names graven there with the pocket edge-tool.
Oh, time has diminished the strength of my spirit;
  The visions of youth are my glories no more;
But still one estate from thee I inherit,
  The old right of way to the stars and their lore.

What eloquence rang from yonder broad staging!
  Old Cicero's spirit was certainly there;
And there was some youthful Demosthenes raging,
  Or Chatham or Webster was sawing the air.
Our essays—the teachers endured them how meekly,
  As well as our sermons on virtue and truth;
But they heard not, as we did, the doggerel weekly,
  The talk of smart fellows and promising youth.

Then the fun of the blunders at each recitation!
  The roasting coal fire beneath the blackboard;
The hard lessons darkening anticipation;
  The way idle scholars were scolded and scored;
The answers from book where the coat-tail concealed it;
  The drawings of genius that stole o'er the slate;
The awkward excuse when a side view revealed it,—
  The broad hint Professor gave lazy-eyed Late.

[75]

And then our Societies,—oh, how we boasted
  Of what we would do and of what we had done:
How oft in debate were our opponents worsted!
  What golden opinions our literature won!
What a fuss we were in at the examination,—
  Pitty-pat went our hearts, and our faces turned red!
What a shout on the stairs, just before the vacation!
  What a funny life through interregnum we led.

Sweet Athens, o'er thee love and light hold dominion!
  They poured their rich harmony full on thy breeze.
Oh, would but some gentle dove lend me his pinions,
  How soon would I perch 'mid thy soft locust trees!
But where is his reverent form who presided,
  Alive with strong intellect, feeling and power!
Whom we loved and revered, and in whom we confided:
  The Washington, guiding through danger's dark
    hour!

Bright Athens, farewell! If thy green slopes should
    never
  Loom up in the distance to welcome me more,
Thy scenes are engrossed on my heart, and forever
  Shall memory faithfully keep them in store.
I think of thy rills, and my blood, richly flowing,
  Leaps freshly as erst through every vein;
And thy landscapes, with distance and time brighter
    growing,
  Seem all made anew in the heavenly plain.

Mr. Emerson died in January, 1891. For many
years his tall figure was a familiar sight on the
streets of Marietta. He walked with the slight
stoop of the scholar and thinker rather than the
alert look of the keen observer. For some time before taking up his residence in Marietta he had lived
in Cincinnati, where he filled a minor political office. He had no visible means of support and seems
to have passed all his time in reading, writing and

reflecting. Small boys occasionally took advantage of his apparent absent-mindedness to play little tricks on him. These unsolicited attentions he always took good-naturedly. Here follows his tribute to

MARIETTA.

Here, where two meeting rivers fringe the plain
O'er which the semicircling green hills tower,
The "Pioneer City" stands: its streets a chain
In graceful folds of cottage, tree and flower.
Here learning loves to build her shady bower,
And like a magnet draws the mind from far,
Giving that mind its own magnetic power,
Freighting the mental and the moral car,
And sprinkling all the West with many a radiant
    star.

It is worth noting, in this connection, that one member of the board objected vigorously though not petulantly to the acceptance of Mr. Emerson's donation on the donor's terms. Although he had probably never heard of Thomas Carlyle, and certainly knew little about him, he shared the rugged Scotchman's aversion to "silly poetry." Henceforth W. D. Emerson's name belongs to the ages; not, it is true, like that of another Emerson, to the whole civilized world, by his writings, but to the comparatively few, who, year after year, will read the catalogue of the O. U. To express the idea by a simile: a thread may be as long as a cable.

When Dr. Leue was secretary of the Ohio Bureau of Forestry he was also a member of the board of trustees of the O. U. He was appointed in 1891. He was a thoroughly competent man, but later got into difficulties in Cincinnati, where he was engaged in school work, that were not to his credit, but upon the merits and demerits of which persons at a distance are not competent to pass just judgment. However, he made strenuous efforts to have a department of forestry established at the college. The archives at Columbus doubtless still contain the bill which he introduced through a member of the Senate, but of which I do not recall the exact date, carrying with it a small appropriation (about $14,000). My recollection is that the bill received fourteen votes, or two less than a majority. Within recent years the need of caring for the forests has begun to dawn upon the minds of legislators all over the country and the situation has received more or less attention in almost every State. It was reported at the time that certain influences in Athens were hostile to the project and were largely responsible for the defeat of the bill. The opposition was due to pure ignorance and stupidity against which even the gods are said to contend in vain. One of the legislators went so far as to say: "Your people don't want this bill passed, why should we interest ourselves in it?"

In June, 1896, president Super offered his resignation to the board to take effect as soon as his successor should be elected, supposing it would require some time and considerable correspondence before a suitable man could be found. Shortly afterwards he started for Europe with a view to placing one of his sons in the University at Jena. Unfortunately, as the event proved, he did not put his written resignation in the hands of the secretary. The man who was appointed temporary president of the board at once called the members together, insisting that the absentee had requested an immediate acceptance of his resignation. No other member had any such information; in fact, it had no existence. The purpose of the deliberate falsehood soon became evident, but it failed completely. When the board met, a contest at once developed between the partisans of two candidates, who were, however, not rivals, neither of whom is now living, that aroused much bitterness. The choice fell upon Dr. Isaac Crook by a small majority. The defeated members did not take their discomfiture with a good grace. Soon conditions developed that made the situation of the president one of extreme difficulty. Under the circumstances it would have been the part of wisdom to secure the goodwill of the faculty. This he failed or neglected or refused to do. Ere long it was currently reported that a "round robin" was circulated among the faculty requesting the board to elect another president. Whether such a document was prepared and if prepared it was placed in the hands of the secretary of the board, the writer does not know. At any rate, president Crook handed in his resignation to take effect at the end of his second year, and it was at once accepted. He was a man of considerable ability, of strict integrity and had had a good deal of experience of various kinds. He was born in Perry County, O., was graduated from the Ohio Wesleyan University and had held pastorates in Ohio, Illinois, Michigan, Missouri and Kentucky. He had been president of the University of the Pacific and chancellor of the University of Nebraska. He was the author of a few books and a frequent contributor to the periodicals of his church. There are persons who maintain that his many moves were due more to a push in the rear than a pull in front. In his latter years he may have consoled himself with the reflections, which other men may have shared with him, that a man may be unsuccessful as the president of a university, a thoroughly competent governor and an outstanding President of the United States. His life extended from 1833 to 1916. One result of president Crook's resignation was perhaps unique in college annals: the predecessor of a president was also his successor. Professor Super of the faculty was again called to the head of the institution, one year as dean and two years as president. He is a Pennsylvanian by birth and a graduate of Dickinson with the class of 1866. Later he taught in Ohio and Delaware and studied in Germany. He visited Europe in all four times for purposes of study and observation. He was a professor of languages in the Cincinnati Wesleyan College from 1872 to '78. The following year he studied law and came to Athens in the autumn of '79 as professor of Greek and German. He has published about a dozen books of varying value. Many of his contributions may be found in newspapers and his name occurs often in the *International Journal of Ethics,* in the *Bibliotheca Sacra,* in the *Popular Science Monthly,* in *Science,* in the *American Antiquarian* and elsewhere. He has also published translations from several modern languages. His first "effusion" appeared in Gettysburg in the fall or winter of 1865. Some of his contributions may also be found in the *Westminster Review* and in other British periodicals. Since his separation from the college several hundred of his communications from his pen have appeared in print and some books that have been highly praised by persons who had not the remotest expectations of profiting by their good words. Whether his life has been a useful one is a question; that it has been strenuous and occasionally breezy, if not tempestuous, does not admit of a doubt.

By 1901 conditions had again become such as to convince the new-old president that his influence, such as he desired it to be, was waning; that a man was wanted who was not obsessed with the "sloppy sentimentality" that it was his duty as a teacher to try to make the world better in however slight a degree, but who would take men as they are. He accordingly again offered his resignation, but under promises that were never fulfilled. Altough elected dean of the college of liberal arts, he was soon made aware that what the new president wanted was not a coadjutor but a sort of "man Friday," who would do what he was ordered to do and ask no questions. Accordingly, a few years later he again offered his resignation, which was accepted against the written protests of four-fifths of the students, and withdrew from all participation in the affairs of the college. He may have thought as did the hen that had inadvertently hatched out a brood of ducklings instead of chicks. When she saw them take to the water and tried to follow, she quickly decided in her rasorial way: *this is no place for me,* and made for the shore with all haste. Then once more was proved the truth of the saying of Homer or of some other ancient or modern poet: "Some men will hold their jobs and some will not." Howbeit, like the Roman

[81]

historian Tacitus, he was fortunate in being permitted to live long enough to witness the return of a better day under the benign influence of an enlightened monarch. The reader is permitted to interpret these somewhat cryptic utterances in such a way as may seem to him best. His successor was a native of Kentucky and occupied the presidency until his death in 1920. He was an alumnus of Miami University, having been a member of the class of '67. He taught in his native State until 1871, when he migrated to Ohio, serving as the head of the schools of Hamilton and Sandusky. In 1892 he was chosen president of the State Agricultural College at Fort Collins, Colo., where he remained until the end of the century, coming to Athens one year later. He took an active part in public and educational affairs both in Colorado and Ohio.

VII*c*

President Super's second successor had an exalted opinion of his qualifications, both physical and intellectual. And he took pains to keep those who came in contact with him duly informed upon these matters. In an educational history of Ohio published near the close of the preceding century, one may read such autobiographical data as the following: "Dr. Ellis has a fine presence and an air of dignity. He is a fine scholar and in logic, economics, civics and history he stands without a rival." None of his predecessors made such a blanket claim to scholarship, or indeed any claim at all. One does not need to belong to the school of the prophets to venture the prediction that none of his successors will place such a high estimate upon himself. According to his own testimony he will always remain in a class by himself, when the roll of his official peers is called, no matter how long it will be. It is surely doing a man no wrong to cite his own estimate of himself. In order to show a due appreciation of Mother Nature's beneficence in fitting him out with a fine presence and an air of dignity he never appeared in public without such artificial adornments as he considered best adapted to supplement her handiwork. He was also equipped with a remarkable fluency of speech—an endowment which he sedulously cultivated. Alas, when the period of silence supervened it came with a tragic suddenness. Many of his acquaintances can testify that his countenance was never "sicklied o'er with the pale cast of thought." Some of those who

were associated with him affirm that his winged
words were never freighted with ideas and that they
were often tipped with barbs of censure that was
not distinguishable from abuse. It is probable that
his atrabilious moods were now and then occasioned
by a chronic malady from which he suffered severely
at times. But it did not keep him from work. Alston Ellis was also firmly convinced that every man
should be his own bellows. Albeit, who will say
that his philosophy of life is unsound? Is not wind
one of nature's most beneficent agencies? It is
only in those rare instances when it becomes too
violent that it brings disaster. And doth not Job
say: "O remember that my life is wind"? Job was
a wise man and no joker. He certainly was in no
facetious mood when he uttered this sentiment. Although our hero had probably never heard of
Aeolus, he would doubtless have been willing to
take upon himself the duties of that ancient but
somewhat mythical potentate. The man who plays
the leading part in such dramas as "The Blowers,"
"The Blowviators," and the "Windians" may make
himself quite interesting, even if his histrionic abilities are not of a high order nor his lungs particularly strong, if he enters with enthusiasm into the
spirit of the production. It may be remarked that
there are now two Caves of the Winds and that
they are no longer in Italy but in Washington,
D. C. Somebody seems to have been of the opinion
that the supply should be doubled.

Naturally there was no lack of carpers and de-
tractors who, prompted by jealousy, as he more than
once publicly asserted, made flippant remarks upon
these matters and otherwise caused him trouble.

Howbeit, he could well afford to ignore such cavillers, for he felt the

> *Justum et tenacum propositi virum*
> *Ne civium ardor prava jubentium.*
>
> . . . .
>
> *Mante quatit solida. . . .**

Equally appropriate in this connection is another Horatian dictum:

> *—populi contemnere voces*
> *Sic solitum: populus me sibilat; at mihi plaudo*
> *Ipse domi, simul ac nummos contemplor in arca.*†

Our worthy president was also a firm believer in the philosophy of life summed up in a saying, usually but erroneously attributed to Sir Robert Walpole, that every man has his price. It is probable that he was not often mistaken. When now and then a member of his entourage showed that he was not amenable to such blandishments, he was almost certain to be made uncomfortable. Furthermore, our president was not only proud of his fluency, he was "puffed up" with his own eloquence. He claimed that during his residence in Colorado he made more speeches than any other man in the centennial State. There are, however, persons still living, and they are not the least discerning, who affirm that his fluency, which they do not deny, was due rather to his facile use of words than to profundity of thought. It may also be asserted with the utmost confidence that to Alston Ellis belongs

* "The man who is upright and steadfast in his purpose can not be turned aside by the clamor of the crowd."

† "Used to despise the hootings of the populace thus: 'The people may hiss me, but I congratulate myself at home when I contemplate the coins in my strong box.'"

A PIONEER COLLEGE

the unique distinction of being the only one of his
official peers who showed the courage necessary to
vindicate his offended dignity by physical force and
prowess. It is true, the mellay did not end as he
intended it should, besides causing him much pain
and no little discomfort but he had consciousness of
feeling that

" 'Tis nobler to have fought and lost,
Than never to have fought at all."

"And Freedom shrieked when Kosciusko fell."

Moreover, as the damage inflicted by his antagonist
was upon that part of his body farthest from his
head it did not impair his efficiency. A few days
after the battle in the president's office one of the
Columbus dailies contained a cartoon in which the
"faithful secretary" was depicted holding up his
hands in holy horror at the tragedy enacted before
his eyes.

"The startled Scriba squeaked when jostled
Alston fell."

The penultimate president of the O. U. has certainly one distinction that is unique. So far as the
writer knows, he is the only member of a college
faculty who has had a building named after him
during his lifetime. Such a thing is sometimes done
to commemorate the gift of a liberal benefactor
while he is yet alive, but for no other reason. There
are persons who profess to see in Ellis Hall the
visible evidence of the nomenclator's powers of persuasion, while others claim that the transaction was
permeated by *arcana* that were not *celestia*.

[86]

"There's no fun in a graveyard,—
I want my flowers now."

Our hero was one of those men for whom, as for the late Stuyvesant Fish, postage-stamp glory had no attractions.

In 1904 occurred a unique event in the history of the O. U.—the centennial of its charter. Mr. George Beaton, a former Athenian but at the time a resident of New York city, provided the means and in conjunction with some of his former friends took the general management of the festivities. He chartered a train in his home city, employed a caterer and transported to Athens all the necessaries for a *fête champetre* on the college campus. The number of guests served was estimated at three thousand, every one of whom was presented with a plate on which was painted a picture of the college building erected in 1817. In the course of the preparations it was demonstrated once more that two men cannot ride the same horse at the same time unless one of them is willing to ride behind. As Mr. Beaton had not only furnished the horse for the occasion and its equipment, at a cost reputed to have been about twenty-five thousand dollars, his friends naturally claimed the right to decide who should be the chief equestrian. To this proposal the head of the college took exception and ultimately refused to participate altogether in the exercises. It is probable that only a few of the people of Athens had knowledge of the collision of interests which the occasion had developed. Nevertheless, it was unfortunate that the literary part of the exercises was almost wholly lacking. Our hero did

[87]

not even manifest the curiosity—or shall we say the interest?—of a certain Zacchaeus, who climbed a sycamore tree, of which there were several on the campus, to observe what was going on below. Rather did he follow the precedent set by a young Greek warrior named Achilles and sulked in his tent because he had not been duly honored by an older warrior named Agamemnon. Albeit, probably few men in this world get their deserts.

" 'Tis true, 'tis pity, and pity 'tis, 'tis true."*

In his attitude toward education the subject of this sketch differed radically with his predecessors and his successors as well. He was a strict utilitarian. He had no patience with idealists. In his chapel talks he frequently told his hearers that he had always held good-paying positions because he had a good education. He despised the man who did not have his eyes always on the "main chance," or who was not first of all a man of affairs. He is reputed to have been very successful in his quest for material gain. Alack and alas, he postponed too long the enjoyment thereof which he promised himself.

"Take him all in all,
We shall not look upon his like again."

If any reader of this sketch is prompted to ask why so much space has been given to one of the

*This episode has reminded the writer of these lines of an incident that occurred in his boyhood days. Several young fellows of the neighborhood decided individually that they would organize a brass band. When they held their first meeting to arrange and to assign to each member his part, three of the youths declared that they would not join unless they were given the bass drum. As this was impossible, the project had forthwith to be abandoned.

THE O. U. BUILDINGS ABOUT '94-5.

presidents of the O. U., he will find the answer implicit in the foregoing quotation. From his point of view his life was by no means a failure. In his later years he was wont to speak rather exultingly of his success in accumulating money. On a certain occasion he said to the writer that he had hardly ever made a bad investment and never one that had caused him serious loss. At the time of his death he was believed to be the wealthiest man in Ohio who had spent nearly all his mature life in school work. He looked forward to the time when he could say: "Soul, thou hast much goods laid up for many years; eat, drink and enjoy thyself." The reader must, however, not assume that there was but one man connected with the board from whom "flashes of silence" were rare and who was never intoxicated with the exuberance of his own verbosity. Not many months had passed after the death of Dr. Ellis when his devoted wife followed him into the realm of the shades and was laid to her final rest by the side of her husband in the mausoleum she had erected only a short time before her passing. Thus the family became extinct.

Upon the sudden death of president Ellis in November, 1920, the trustees appointed Dean Chubb of the College of Liberal Arts President *ad interim*. Edwin Watts Chubb is a native of eastern Pennsylvania and a graduate of Lafayette College of the class of 1887. He studied one year in the University of Berlin, taught in his native State and in Wisconsin, coming to the O. U. in 1900. He is the author of a number of books and a contributor to American periodicals. Unostentatiously and without the blare of trumpets or campaign promises, he took hold of the situation intelligently, among other things contributing not a little to the enactment of the Fouts bill mentioned in another part of this volume. His successor was elected in midsummer, 1922. With the accession of Elmer Burritt Bryan to the presidency of the college the office came again to an Ohioan, although as in the case of Solomon Howard by a narrow margin, as he is a native of Van Wert. He is a graduate of Indiana University, did post-graduate work at Harvard and Clark Universities, taught in various high schools, was a professor in Butler College and president of Franklin College until 1909, when he was chosen head of Colgate University. During the years 1901-3 he was principal of the Insular High School in the Philippines. He has published a number of books and pamphlets on the principles and practice of education.

The present numerical status of the university is taken from the catalogue of 1922-3

Students in the College of Liberal Arts, including those in the College of Arts and of Music.... 794
Students in the College of Education 355
Students in the two-years course 489

Total 1,638

Total for the two summer terms, 1922......... 1,746
Total registration for the University extension course 1,211

The 1,638 students were thus distributed:
College of Liberal Arts, Men................ 483
Women 306
College of Education, Men 138
Women 706

Not only is the O. U. no longer a youngster, it is a vigorous oldster. If the disembodied spirit of Manasseh Cutler and of not a few others who "died without the sight" take any account of things mundane, it must surely give them great joy to realize that their labors were not in vain. It is probable, however, that the self-denial of the founders was not less than that of not a few men who were engaged in giving instruction in later years. The number of names on the university pay-roll is about one hundred and fifty.

Dr. Cutler's last years were much embittered by the reflection that his labors and self-denial in the establishment of his Western University were not appreciated or even recognized. There is no room here to consider his case, but it must be said of a truth that the charge cannot be justly brought against the present generation or its immediate predecessors.

VIII

In this section will be given biographical sketches of several men who, in recent years, were connected with the college either as students or as teachers. Owing to the exigencies of space the names must be few and most of the sketches brief. An exceptionally tragic element was brought into the history of the O. U., although somewhat at long range, by its first professor of pedagogy. John P. Gordy was born near Salisbury, Md., in 1851. He was graduated from the Connecticut Wesleyan University in 1878. For several years he was an instructor in his *alma mater* and in 1884 received the degree of Ph. D. from the University of Leipzig and that of LL. D. from the University of Pennsylvania in 1891. He was a member of the O. U. faculty from 1886 until 1896. Thereafter until his death he held chairs in the State University at Columbus and in New York University. Upon the rather sudden demise of their only daughter who was born in Athens, he and his wife seem to have made a suicide pact; at any rate, they were found dead together shortly after the sad event. Dr. Gordy was the translator of Kuno Fischer's "Descartes" and the author of some volumes on psychology and pedagogy. His small manual entitled "Elements of Psychology" was highly praised by some of the most competent authorities. He left an uncompleted "History of Political Parties in the United States." He had also prepared, under the auspices of William T. Harris who was then at the head of the Bureau of Education in Washington, a "His-

tory of Normal Schools in the United States."
Notwithstanding some idiosyncrasies, he was well
liked by his students and his career at the O. U. was
greatly to its advantage. Dr. Gordy was strangely
reticent about his past life. The writer never saw
a photograph of him and there is reason to believe
that none exists. During his first year at the O. U.
we had many discussions and long conversations
about his work and matters in general. Yet I
never learned from him that he had been brought
up on a farm, nor anything about his student life
in this country and in Germany, except in the most
general way, nor about his experience as a teacher
in common schools, nor about his career as a teacher
in his *alma mater*. His marriage to an American
woman in Germany was never alluded to. Dr.
Gordy's chief merit as a teacher lay in his intellectual penetration. He knew by a sort of instinct
how to stimulate the minds of his students. He
often said that the mistake made by most instructors of youth and young people was their failure
to get the right point of view; that they usually assumed too much knowledge on their part and therefore failed to interest. He maintained that the
number of young persons who could not be interested in anything was very small, and that every
subject could be made attractive if properly han-
dled by the instructor. He was endowed with such
a profound penetration of fundamentals in pedagogy that he was able to grasp the essentials of a
subject of which he did not know very much. Not
long after the departure of Dr. Gordy from the
O. U. a member of the faculty received a letter from
a former student in which the writer said, in part:

[93]

"I spent most of the summer at the St. Louis Exposition. I heard most of the lectures delivered by distinguished men from all parts of the world. I made the acquaintance of many of them and had frequent conversations with several. Yet in all the notable company I did not meet with one whom I considered the equal of two men to whom I recited at the O. U. One of those men was Professor Gordy." In my conversation with him on various matters it came about now and then that mention was made of the uncertainty of life and of our inability to predict when the final summons would come. He generally closed the discussion with the remark: "I have no use for death." The strangeness and premeditatedness of the dual suicide created a veritable sensation all over the country, but particularly among the friends of the family in New York city. The question is pertinent whether the parents of Miss Gordy believed that "death ends all," so that when their daughter had passed from life the event made a stay upon earth no longer worth while, or whether they believed that she had entered into the realm of spirits and wished to be with her as soon as possible. Dr. Gordy was a very impulsive man. It is therefore probable that under the awful burden of his overwhelming sorrow a further stay among the living looked so dark and cheerless that he decided to cut it short at once. But we may well ask, why did not the parents of Miss Gordy use their means to erect a monument to their daughter, which, although invisible and intangible, in a certain sense, would continue to benefit at least a small portion of mankind for all time to come? Their bereavement was by no means without precedent.

One of the first innovations after Dr. Gordy became a member of the faculty was the introduction of vocal music and drawing into the curriculum. This was possible only by persuading the school board to share the expense of a teacher who could give instruction in both branches. There was, however, considerable objection to this arrangement on the ground that it was an unnecessary innovation. Albeit, the situation gradually cleared itself and each party employed its own instructor. Later, instrumental music and voice culture were added to the course until the number of teachers amounted to nearly a dozen and the number of pianos to nearly two score. Then followed courses in business or commerce. To this arrangement some of the alumni objected, fearing lest it would degrade the college to the level of a short-course commercial school. It was argued, on the other hand, that as a large part of every progressive community is engaged in business there is abundant justification for giving it a place in a liberal education. Not many years had passed until this fact was generally recognized and one short-course commercial college after another ceased to exist, being absorbed by the regular colleges and universities. So successful was this special training that for a time comparatively few of those who took it remained in college long enough to earn a degree because they were drawn into profitable employment. Soon after Dr. Gordy entered upon his duties a Training School was put in operation, a course of study laid out corresponding to that in vogue in most state normal schools in the country and requiring somewhat more work than the existing preparatory department. Those completing this course were given a certificate of proficiency but no degree. Some of those who had completed this short course later re-entered college and finished the work necessary to a degree. The degree of A. M. or of Ph. D. was likewise granted to a few persons upon examination. All these steps were more or less vigorously opposed by the conservatives on the ground that such things had never been done before. The same objections were used that Columbus encountered when he proposed to discover land by sailing westward from Europe. It was the same argument that was adduced against Fulton when he proposed to propel boats by steam. It was the same argument that so great a man in his day as Dr. Dionysius Lardner used to prove, *a priori,* that no ship could be driven across the Atlantic by steam power. He lived long enough to see the error of his way. Conservatism has its merits, but its demerits are still greater. Old Well Enough is not a bad fellow, but he is lazy or at least averse from directing his efforts towards an end that is not in plain sight by means with which he is familiar. Even after men have been persuaded that a new thing should and could be done there are always a few who insist in doing it in the old way. Some days after a "Yankee" had introduced a few wheelbarrows into China he found four of the "Chinks" carrying the new-fangled contrivance.

For some years the college issued a Bulletin from time to time containing papers by students and members of the faculty. Persons who are interested in the gradual development and expansion of the O. U. can trace its course by an examination of the successive catalogues and bulletins. Before Dr.

Scott had resigned he had secured, with no little difficulty, two different appropriations from the legislature amounting to twenty thousand dollars for the repair of the buildings and the erection of a chapel. This money was used for raising the roof of the Center Building and the erection of a chapel. The chapel was placed upon the site of the present Ewing Hall. It was large enough to accommodate two hundred persons on the first floor and the same number in two rooms on the second. After the means had been provided by the Sleeper Bill for a large building it became evident to the board that the site occupied by the structure erected about a dozen years before was its proper location. A contract was accordingly entered into with a Chicago firm for removing the "Old Chapel" to its present location. This rather difficult feat was accomplished without difficulty or delay. Now, enclosed in its mantle of ivy, it is the most picturesque building on the campus.

C. L. Martzloff was of Alsatian ancestry. For the last five years of his life he had been in rather feeble health, but stuck to his post almost to the end. For several years he had been at the head of the department of history in the College of Liberal Arts and secretary of the Alumni Association. He received two degrees from the O. U. and in 1920 that of Litt. D. from Wittenberg College. He wrote a number of articles, pamphlets and books mostly pertaining to the history of Ohio. Probably no man of his age—53—was more familiar with this subject than Professor Martzloff. Yet he was no bookworm, but took an active interest in the political, religious and moral affairs of the community, of his State and of his church. In 1911-12 he was chairman of the Democratic committee of his native county (Perry). He was a delegate to several State conventions and a Wilson elector in 1912. He was once defeated for the National House of Representatives on the Democratic ticket. This had been the fate of his predecessors for many years. He was a fluent and forcible speaker. Among his departed friends there is none whom the writer of these lines misses more sadly and whose untimely demise he more deeply deplores than that of Clement Luther Martzloff. There have doubtless been as good men as he even in Athens; but not as many as the world needs. It is a sad fatality that the department of history lost a predecessor who, like him, could ill be spared, professor B. O. Higley. Of no two men could it more truly be said that they did what they could to make this world a better place to live in. Professor Higley died in April, 1905, and Professor Martzloff, on the fifth of August, 1922.

The second man formerly connected with the O. U. whose life went out in a tragedy in the twentieth century was Professor C. W. Waggoner. He was born in Hocking County, Ohio, and received his Bachelor's degree in 1904. He then entered Cornell University, where he received his Master's degree the following year. He was an instructor in the same institution until 1909, when he received the degree of Doctor of Philosophy. Shortly afterwards he was given an appointment in the University of West Virginia as an instructor in physics and was later appointed as head of the department. He was granted leave of absence for the year

1922-3 and went to Shreveport, La., to make some investigations. He was killed by being thrown from a horse. Of Dr. Waggoner, one of his colleagues said that he was an "original investigator, an inspiring teacher, an enthusiastic leader and a faithful friend. He will be missed in all the activities of the university and the city." Another wrote: "Dr. Waggoner was, in the minds of the students, the most loved and the most respected man connected with the university. He was often referred to as 'the best friend the students have.' He was always more concerned with the welfare of the students than with his own. Those who knew him in his classes, or in the Sunday School, had the most genuine love for him. All knew him as the squarest of men. No other death could have caused more profound grief to the student body." Mrs. Waggoner was also, for a time, a member of the faculty of the O. U. In a letter written to her shortly after the accident that took her husband's life, a prominent chemist pays his tribute to the deceased: "I am sixty years old and have known many people; but in all my life I have never known another man so useful and of such promise for future usefulness to mankind in general."

Among the persons whose ideas have, for many years, attracted the attention of the world's leading thinkers is a man whose name is known to comparatively few. A recent issue of the *Toronto Globe*, after commenting on the extraordinary efforts of the *New York Times* to furnish the public with early and accurate information, continues: "During the World War, too, its enterprise in getting news was readily in evidence. Large sums of money were expended in wireless and cable communications and the *Times* warrantably boasted of excluding advertising matter from its pages to permit of the publication of important cable news. And the man to whom the largest share of praise is due for the enterprise, the conscientiousness and the uniformly high quality which has marked its news service is Mr. Carr V. Van Anda, the managing editor. The accuracy of his measure of the value of the news and of the requirements of the reading public have elevated him to a high place in the world of journalism." Mr. Van Anda was born in Georgetown, Ohio, in 1864. He attended the O. U. in 1880-2. After being employed in various capacities on the *Cleveland Herald,* the *Baltimore Sun* and the *New York Sun,* he was transferred to the *Times* in 1904, which position he has since held. In 1920 the O. U. honored itself and him by conferring upon him the honorary degree of LL. D.

It is probable that if an expert were to select from the alumni and former students of the O. U. that one who has been seen and heard by more people than any other, the choice would fall upon S. W. Gillilan. Mr. Gillilan had done some newspaper work as early as 1888, before he entered the University. Later he was on the staff of the *Telegram* of Richmond (Ind.) and the *Palladium* of the same city. In 1901-2 he was connected with the Los Angeles *Herald* and in 1902-5 with the *Baltimore American*. He also contributed to the *Chicago Daily News* and the *Baltimore Sun*. For about twenty years he has been much in demand as a Lyceum lecturer and has written some volumes that are widely read.

AND ITS BACKGROUND

The writer of this brief biography has sometimes wondered whether "Strick" now and then recalls the occasion when he was cited before a member of the faculty to answer for some peccadillo of which he was rather more than suspected of being guilty, on which occasion he assured his cross-examiner that he had been doing his best to make the boys conduct themselves decently and in order, but in vain. You can't whitewash a house with yellow paint. Notwithstanding his little faults, "Strick" was, and I suppose still is, a good fellow. There was not a particle of malice in his psyche.

The General Education Board recently announced its intention to extend its work already inaugurated so as to coöperate with State and City departments. Dr. Frank P. Bachman has been appointed director of the division. The appointee is a native of Illinois and an A. B. of the University of Chicago. He spent one year at Marburg in Germany and received his doctor's degree at Columbia in 1902. From 1902 to 1908 he was professor of education at the O. U. Later, after serving three years as Assistant Superintendent of the Cleveland public schools, he was appointed educational expert to the Board of Estimates of New York city and still later to membership on the Rockefeller Board. Partly alone and partly in collaboration he has published several books and reports.

Clyde Brown was a member of the class of '95. His name appears in the college catalogue as one of the instructors between 1893 and 1901; in the later period as professor of philosophy and pedagogy. During these years he studied law, afterwards practicing in Philadelphia and New York, where he still resides as general solicitor for the New York Central lines. He is credited with receiving a larger salary than any other alumnus of the O. U., living or dead. Mr. Brown had more to do with the enactment of the Sleeper Bill into a law than any other man who was not a member of the General Assembly. Although "Brown" is one of the commonest family names in Anglo-Saxondom, there is at least one Brown who is no common man; and he is no longer a resident of Ohio. Mrs. Brown is also a graduate of the O. U., having been a member of the class of '96.

Henry W. Elson was born in Muskingum County, O., in 1857. He graduated from Thiel College and later from the Lutheran Theological Seminary in Philadelphia. He did post-graduate work in the Uunversity of Pennsylvania and subsequently held pastorates in the same State. For some time he was a lecturer and writer for the University Extension Society of Philadelphia. For eleven years preceding 1916 he was professor of ecomonics and history in the O. U. In the latter year he was elected president of Thiel College, but soon after resigned said position in order to devote himself entirely to the writing of books mainly such as dealt with the history of the United States. Some of Dr. Elson's books are widely read. Dr. Elson was also a member of the Ohio constitutional convention of 1912.

Charles H. Grosvenor came to Athens from Connecticut when five years old in 1838. He was admitted to the bar in 1857. He entered the Union army in 1861 and rose to the rank of brigadier-general. He was a member of the Ohio House of Representatives, 1874-8, and speaker one term. He was a member of Congress from 1885 to 1907 less one term. He died in 1917. Although never a student in the college, he is mentioned here for the reason that he was mainly instrumental in securing for it and the city the Carnegie library. It stands on the college campus and is one of its ornaments. General Grosvenor's successor in Congress, although not immediate, the Hon. I. M. Foster, is a graduate of the local college. He belongs to the class of '95. Like his predecessor, he is of New England ancestry but more remote.

William E. Henderson is a native of western Pennsylvania. He received his A. B. and his A. M. from Wooster College and his Ph. D. from the Johns Hopkins University. He was later a professor in Emporia, Kansas, fellow in chemistry at the Johns Hopkins University and professor of chemistry at the O. U. for two years beginning with 1897. Since that time he has been connected with the State University at Columbus, being at present dean of the College of Liberal Arts. He has published about half a dozen textbooks dealing with different departments of chemistry. It was recently reported by persons who are perhaps inclined to be somewhat irreverent that the department of liberal arts at the Columbus institution being a mere lean-to or side-show for the main circus, Dr. Henderson was considered the best qualified member of the faculty to assume the responsibility for this department in addition to his own. Howbeit, in this case as in many others, it is well and wise to keep in mind the dictum that we should use discretion in finding fault with one thing because it is not something else. What the attitude of the present board is towards the culture studies the writer does not know. That some at least of their predecessors were indifferent or even hostile is no secret. To them a scythe or a sickle was of more importance than a stradivarius.

James E. Le Rossignol was born in the Province of Quebec. At McGill University he made a brilliant record and received his A. B. degree in 1888, at the age of 22. In '92 he was given the degree of Ph. D. by the University of Leipzig and later in the same year became a Fellow at Clark University. During 1892-4 he was professor of ethics and psychology at the O. U. Then the state of his health made it imperative for him to seek another climate. Fortunately an opening presented itself in the University of Denver, where he remained seventeen years. There he was elected Director of the School of Commerce of the University of Nebraska. At various times he has also been special lecturer in his *alma mater*, at the University of Wisconsin and elsewhere. In the latter half of 1906 he studied economic conditions in New Zealand. He has published "Monopolies," "Orthodox Socialism," "Little Stories of Quebec," "State Socialism in New Zealan," "Jean Baptiste," besides a number of monographs on economic subjects.

Carl Leo Mees was born in Columbus in 1853. He was a student in the State University in 1874-5. In the latter year he received the degree of M. D. He did post-graduate work in Berlin and in the South Kensington museum. After filling temporarily several other positions, he occupied the chair of physics in the O. U. from 1882 to 1887. For some years he was a pofessor of physics in the Rose Polytechnic Institute and later president of the

THE NEW GYMNASIUM

Outside the campus close to Lindley Hall

same until 1919, when he was made president emeritus. He is the author of many scientific papers.

William F. Peirce was born at Chicopee Falls, Mass., in 1868. He received his A. B. from Amherst College in 1888 and A. M. in '92. Hobart College granted him the degree of L. H. D. and two other colleges that of D. D. He was professor of psychology and pedagogy at the O.U. in 1891-2 and for four years professor of ethics and phychology at Kenyon College. Since 1896 he has been president of the same institution.

Frank H. H. Roberts was born in Knox County in 1869. He received his bachelor's degree from the O. U. in '92 and his A. M. from Kenyon College in '99. For some years he was engaged in school and newspaper work in his native State. From 1899 to 1903 he was principal of the Wyoming State Normal School, and from the latter date to 1914 he was professor of history in the University of Denver. Until recently he has been president of the New Mexico Normal University. He has been a lecturer at various Chautauquas. He was director of the Wyoming exhibit at the Paris exposition in 1900 and first director of the Wyoming exhibit at the St. Louis exhibition in 1904. In 1915 he was sent to Europe by the trustees of Denver University to investigate municipal ownership. In 1916 and 1920 he was a delegate to the Methodist General Conference. He is at present a member of the International World Movement and one of its executive committee. He has delivered frequent lectures in English and Spanish besides contributing to various periodicals. He has published: "A Comparative Study of State and Municipal Government," Civil Government in Wyoming," "History and Civics of New Mexico," and the "Constitution of Colorado." His present address is El Paso, Texas.

The intelligent reader of this volume, "if any such there be," can hardly help arriving at the conclusion that no other municipality, so small at least in the "West," is the birthplace or the educatrix or both, of so many men who left their impress on the affairs of the nation and especially upon the Protestant Church, Methodist Episcopal branch, as Athens, O. Some of the names occurring on the following pages have already been mentioned, but their careers merit a fuller notice. Furthermore, owing to the fact that the scene on which our little drama was acted is comparatively limited and owing to the further fact that a few of the original actors appear in different rôles, occasional repetitions are essential to the comparative completeness of our story; they have not therefore been meticulously avoided. Three bishops were born in the village while a fourth was a native of the county. Three were students in the local college, of whom two remained long enough to earn a degree.

Some of the distinctively denominational institutions have educated a larger number of ecclesiastical leaders, but no territory so small has given birth to so many. Bishop Ames was born in the township that still bears the family name. The earliest member of the Ames family in Ohio was Silvanus, who was born in Massachusetts in 1771. His father had been a chaplain in the revolutionary army and died at Valley Forge from the effects of the hard winter of 1777-78. Silvanus migrated into Ohio, or rather into the Northwest Territory, in 1798, settling first at Belpre on the Ohio River opposite Parkersburg, W. Va., but moving on to a farm in what is now Ames township, Athens County, in 1800. At the time of his death he had held almost every office in the county and was an acknowledged leader in southeastern Ohio. Bishop Ames was the third son of Silvanus. For a few terms he was a student in the O. U. He was elected and consecrated bishop in Boston in 1852. Bishop MacCabe, although an Athenian by birth, was never a student in the college. His life covered the period from 1836 to 1906. He served for a time as a chaplain in the northern army during our sectional war, was captured and confined in Libby prison, and later detailed his experience in that gloomy abode to large audiences. In 1896 he was consecrated bishop and during his last years was Chancellor of the University at Washington, D. C.

E. H. Moore was born in Boylston, Massachusetts, in 1812, and came to Athens with his parents in 1816. He was mainly self-educated, but learned surveying under the tutelage of S. B. Pruden, by whom he was appointed deputy surveyor in 1836. Later he was elected to the office of county surveyor and was twice re-elected. In 1868 he was elected to the national Congress, but declined a re-election. He was a trustee of the O. U. from 1861 to the time of his death in 1900, and treasurer from 1875 until 1897. During all his mature life Mr. Moore was greatly interested in the welfare of the community, of the State and of the nation. It was mainly through his untiring efforts that the Southeastern Ohio Hospital for the

Insane was located near the county seat. His only
son, David Hastings Moore, a classmate of Earl
Cranston, for a number of years held pastorates in
the church of his choice. Later he was president of
the Cincinnati Wesleyan Female College and still
later chancellor of the University of Denver. While
occupying this position he was elected bishop in
1910. The bishop's oldest son, who bears his grand-
father's name Eliakim Hastings, has long been a
professor of mathematics in the University of Chicago. Samuel B. Pruden was born near Morris-
town, N. J. His family came to Athens in 1815.
One of his daughters married John Brough, who
was afterward elected governor of Ohio. He had
been a student for a short time at the O. U. Mr.
Pruden's wife was Mary Cranston, an aunt of Earl
Cranston. He was a trustee of the O. U. from
1851 to the time of his death in 1862. He held at
different times offices in the county and was for
many years one of its leading citizens. The Cranston family came to Athens from western New
York during the War of 1812-14. There were two
sons and several daughters. They came down the
Ohio on a flat-boat to the mouth of the Hocking
River, thence upstream on a craft or raft built for
the purpose. Most of the family walked along the
bank while their belongings were "poled upstream"
on the water; the mother and a babe were carried
on horseback. The trunk of a large sycamore tree
that had fallen on their track furnished shelter for
the family during one rainy night. Mary Cranston's husband, the Samuel Pruden mentioned
above, had a salt-boiling establishment a mile or
more east of Athens. Two of Mr. Pruden's sons

were among the first students at the O. U. The boiling of salt was an important industry in the early days of Ohio and in fact of almost the entire western territory until near the end of the nineteenth century. Earl Cranston's father having died before his son's birth, the child's training devolved upon his step-father, J. W. Longbon of Jackson, Ohio. He seems to have discharged his duty with exemplary fidelity. Young Cranston graduated from the O. U. in 1861 and entered the Union army soon after. He saw considerable service in Virginia, but resigning on account of ill health he began the study of law. But soon feeling irresistibly drawn to the Christian ministry he entered the Ohio Conference of the Methodist Episcopal Church in 1867. He rose rapidly and after filling a number of important positions he was elected bishop in 1896. At present he is the sole surviving member of the Episcopal quartet born in Athens county.

Joseph M. Trimble, a son of Governor Allen Trimble of Ohio, was born in Woodford County, Ky. In 1807 he entered the O. U. at the age of sixteen and received his degree in 1823. Soon after his graduation he was admitted to the Ohio Conference of the Methodist Episcopal Church and served as its secretary for thirty-one years—more than twice as long as any of his successors. In 1833 young Trimble was appointed professor in Augusta College, an institution that we have met more than once in the course of this narrative. That position he held for five years. In his later years he was probably the most widely known member of the Ohio Conference. He was twelve times elected to membership in the General Conference, beginning with that of 1844. He also held important positions in his church besides those just mentioned.

It will be proper here to give some brief biographical sketches of men who were more or less closely identified with the early history of the O. U. and to add a few data to those already recorded.

Some of the names occurring on the following pages have already been mentioned but a fuller account of the careers of their bearers will not be superfluous.

It is an established fact that Manasseh Cutler and his fellow citizen Nathan Dane, a graduate of Harvard, were the principal authors of the Ordinance of 1787. The former was unquestionably the most widely read member of the group with which he coöperated. He was born in 1742 and graduated from Yale College in 1765. He was a chaplain in the Revolutionary army, a member of the Colonial legislature, of the National Congress, a practicing physician and a scientist of considerable note for his day. He received the honorary degree of D. D. from his *alma mater* in 1789. He was also a member of the American Academy of Sciences, of the Masaschusetts Historical Society and an honorary member of the Massachusetts Medical Society. In 1788, after the Pilgrims had made some progress with their new settlement at the mouth of the Muskingum, Dr. Cutler spent a few weeks among them and to the end of his days continued to manifest an interest in their welfare. He died in 1820. In a letter to General Putnam dated June 3, 1800, he makes it clear that he had pondered deeply the problem involved in the founding of the proposed university. He writes among other things that, as an American Congress had made the grant of land, no name appeared to him more appropriate than "American University." "I hope the name will not be changed." (The name was not changed; it was simply displaced by another.) Dr. Cutler had also considered the title "Western University." We have already seen, in the sketch of Dickinson College, and here we find again what limited views, in those days, men had of what was connoted by the term "western." A weekly newspaper published in Cincinnati is still called the "Western Christian Advocate," while one issued in St. Louis is denominated the "Central Advocate." Dr. Cutler also devised the plan by which he desired the university to be governed. He thinks it should not only have a president but a vice-president also. He is of the opinion that the trustees should live near the college and also on the college lands. His ideas about limiting the income of an institution of higher learning are so puerile as to be almost incredible. "If your assembly (legisalture) would not be likely to make any limit it might be best not to say anything about it. But if they will do it, I am certain that forty or fifty thousand dollars would not be too high, as it must be applied to one of the most useful and important purposes to government and to society. The sum sounds large, but no one can tell to what amount the income of this university will arrive in the end." If a large city had grown up on any part of the college lands the reverend gentleman's most sanguine possibility might have been realized. As events shaped themeslves the realization came about in another way. A century after Cutler's death his *alma mater* had an endowment of several million dollars which is steadily growing. The present financial condition of the O. U. is briefly set forth elsewhere in this volume. Dr. Cutler's "right hand man" was Rufus Putnam, the founder of Marietta, the first settlement of whites in Ohio. He was born in Massachusetts in 1738. Although almost entirely self-taught, he distinguished himself in later life as a military officer, as a surveyor, as a legislator and as a judge. He was the personal leader of the first band of white settlers who made the journey to the "far west," although it was far from New England only. The company, after a laborious passage across the Alleghanies, arrived at Marietta, or rather upon the site thereof, on the seventh day of April, 1788. The following year General Putnam was appointed judge of the Supreme Court of the district. He took an active part in the formation of a Bible Society and was its first president. He appears to have had every qualification of the patriotic citizen, of the far-seeing statesman and of the honest and honorable man. On the outward journey he exercised the supreme command, and also in the infant colony until the arrival of General St. Clair. He was a trustee of the O. U. until his death in 1824. He was the last surviving general who held commands during the War of the Revolution. In his correspondence appears for the first time, so far as is known, the suggestion that Congress, which had at its disposal an abundance of land and of debts and no money with which to pay them, should provide endowments for education with public lands. Benjamin Tupper appears to have been his most zealous co-laborer. An interesting and illuminating parallel might be traced between the educational ideas and ideals of Franklin and Putnam.* At the time when the University of Pennsylvania received its official designation there was no similar institution in this country. The initial idea was conceived in the fertile brain of Franklin and set forth in a pamphlet published by him. The institution was chartered in 1750. It was a grandiose project and was very slowly carried out and put into execution. Franklin, like Putnam, was entirely self-taught. Very little was known in this country of European universities, except those of England and Scotland, until several years after the beginning of the last century. Harvard is generally supposed to be the oldest institution of "higher learning" in the New World. It was long preceded by at least one in South America. It should, however, always be kept in mind that "higher learning" is a very elastic term. Everything depends upon what is below. When about twenty years old Franklin worked for some time in England, perhaps all the time in London, and it may be taken for granted that he informed himself upon the means for promoting higher education in that country. Elementary education can hardly be said to have existed. It certainly received very little consideration.

Doubtless the first alumnus of the O. U. who in

* George Haven Putnam, the octogenarian publisher and successful business man, the organizer of the American Copyright League, of the English Speaking Union, an advocate of free trade and the League of Nations, an enthusiastic devotee to terrestrial and aquatic athletics, and the writer of a dozen books, also a Major in the Civil war, has recorded in his latest "Memories" some interesting facts regarding his remote ancestor, Rufus Putnam, a leader in the Colonial wars and in the war of the Revolution.

[113]

later life achieved a nation-wide reputation was Thomas Ewing. He was the son of George Ewing, a native of New Jersey. As a lieutenant in the Colonial army he participated in the battle of Monmouth, the same engagement which may be said to have made Moll Pitcher famous. One of his sisters married Captain John Morgan, who was for many years a member of the Virginia House of Burgesses. Thomas Ewing was born in Ohio County, Virginia. Shortly after this event the family moved into the Buckeye State and settled near Waterford, which at that time was garrisoned by about fifteen men and known as Fort Frye. In 1912 Professor Martzloff published in the twenty-first volume of the Ohio State Archæological and Historical Society the brief autobiography of Mr. Ewing with a number of explanatory notes. This autobiography was afterwards issued in pamphlet form. A few brief extracts are here given, chiefly for the purpose of affording the reader an insight into the conditions amid which young Ewing passed his early life and of showing the extraordinary ability with which the future statesman was endowed. The document also gives us an insight into the humble beginning of the O. U. "My father's little cabin was about fourteen miles from any habitation and so remained during this year. I was then about eight years old and I had no playmates. In the spring of 1802, as I think but I cannot be certain, ten or fifteen of our neighbors united and raised a fund with which to buy books. I contributed ten raccoon skins, being all my hoarded wealth. One of the neighbors, Samuel Brown, was going to Boston and he took charge of the fund. (John Jacob Astor had already engaged in the fur business.) We got some sixty or seventy volumes tolerably well selected—they were brought from Marietta on horseback and emptied out on the floor at Captain Benjamin Brown's, where I was present to witness the exhibition. It seemed to me an almost unbounded intellectual treasury—the library of the Vatican and all other libraries of which I had read were trifles, playthings, compared with it." In 1809 young Ewing made his way by flat-boat to the Kanawha salt-works near the town of Point Pleasant, where he remained three months, receiving good wages as a laborer. This place is somewhat noted in American history as the scene of a battle fought in 1774 between the Colonial troops and the Indians. The forces were about equal—a thousand on a side—but the Red Men withdrew, thus acknowledging defeat. As a result of the fight, the Indians relinquished all claim to territory north of the Ohio River. There is in the town a monument to Cornstalk, who was the leader of the Red Men. "The next year I went to the college at Athens to try my success as a scholar. (The O. U. had been opened in the same year that Ewing went to Virginia. Its initial enrollment was three students.) I mastered the English grammar in ten days, never having previously studied it. But I was familiar with the best English authors and spoke and wrote as correctly before as after." (Might he not have written: "I spoke and wrote as correctly after as before"?) "The seventy-six rules of Adam's Latin Grammar I committed to memory in a single day; still it required many days to study and find the rules always at hand and ready of application." "In 1813 I went home, took with me a

Virgil, a Latin dictionary and grammar and went
on with my studies there, commencing with the
Aeneid, because, being a narrative, it was easier for
a beginner than the Bucolics and the Georgics. I
laid my watch on the table before me and worked
by the hour, doubling instead of anticipating the
eight-hour day. The first day I made but sixty
lines; the last, twelve hundred. And I so read as
to fully comprehend the meaning of every sen-
tence.* The exact date of Mr. Ewing's birth is
uncertain. His father recorded the event as having
taken place on the twentieth of December, 1789,
while his mother insisted that the true date was the
day before Christmas. Professor Martzloff cor-
rected some palpable errors into which the lapse of
time had led Mr. Ewing. These are, however, matters of minor importance; what is important is the
insight it gives into pioneer conditions in Ohio,
not withstanding the fact that Mr. Ewing's kindly
nature prompted him to write more favorably of
some men than they deserved. A committee appointed by the board of trustees from their own
number, there being no organized faculty at the
time, recommended, after due examination, that
Thomas Ewing and John Hunter be given the degree of Bachelor of Arts and Science. As candidates for degrees were, for some time, examined by
trustees, it is probable that they furnished more fun

* It is related of Mr. Ewing that, in later life, having taken
charge of an important law case in which a knowledge of the
Spanish language was essential, and that, either because he had
difficulty in finding a trustworthy interpreter, or what is more
probable, considered such a functionary superfluous, set to
work to learn the language, and that after two weeks' study
had gained such a mastery of the Castilian as to make an interpreter unnecessary.

[116]

than fright. They certainly did if they were of the same caliber with those to which the writer has listened. The date of the diplomas is May 3, 1815. As a large part of Mr. Ewing's life was devoted to the service of his country, we are not further concerned with it here. But the following excerpt from a letter written by Theodore Jervey, author of a life of Hayne, is worthy of insertion. "From one of my friends I first heard of this great son of Ohio. But I have other reasons for being interested in Ewing. I note that he graduated one year prior to that which saw Hayne of South Carolina win his election to the State Legislature. Fifteen years later you note Ewing in the United States Senate, where he found Hayne had preceded him by seven years. Hayne met in debate in the Senate many strong men, Clay, Webster, Dickerson and Chambers; but I do not think any man he ever met in debate helped him so much as Ewing. Ewing's speech in 1832 was the strongest presentation made in reply to Hayne, and this despite the fact that Clay made a famous speech. Ewing's ideas reappear in an address by Hayne delivered some five or six years later when he was exerting every effort of which he was capable to put through the railroad to connect Ohio and South Carolina, etc."

The Rev. Jacob Young, who was Presiding Elder of the district to which Athens belonged, gives us a glimpse of the early days of the college. Writing about 1833-4 he thus expresses himself: "When I visited Athens, what is now called the college green was covered with lofty trees and the surrounding country was almost in a state of nature. There were a few cabins inhabited by hunters, but even in that early day I met with a few men of energy and enterprise who were doing well for themselves, their country and their families. I was at the time charmed with the scenery that surrounded the place, and I thought it might one day vie with ancient Athens. I left the place and was absent about twelve years and when I was returning I expected to see the place greatly improved—at least a flourishing college and a well-arranged academy under the supervision of a good principal and well-selected teachers; but in all these things I was somewhat disappointed. They had a school there called a college, kept in a kind of antiquated building. The walls of the hall looked more like the walls of a prison than a college. The Hon. Thomas Ewing was then going to college there. He said to me: 'It is a place where a young man can study successfully, but it is a poor place to gain instruction.' But I suppose the men who had charge of the school were doing the best they could, and I must tread lightly on the ashes of the dead." Mr. Ewing's idea of the situation seems to mean that there was a considerable collection of books accessible to the students, but that the instruction was inferior. The building to which Mr. Young refers is described in another part of this volume. Mr. Ewing did not attend school in any of the buildings now standing.

George Ewing was evidently somewhat of a restless character; for in 1818 he migrated to Perry County, Indiana, a location that could be reached by flatboat on the Ohio River from him home on the Muskingum. His son Thomas began the study of law and was admitted to the bar in Lancaster

in 1816. Judge Sherman, with whom he studied,
was an important member of the bar until his sudden death at Lebanon in 1829. His name appears
on Mr. Ewing's diploma, as the O. U. had no faculty at that date. He was the father of eleven
children, of whom William T., born in 1820, was
the sixth and John, perhaps equally well known
with his elder brother, was the eighth. The Sherman children having been left orphans, as we have
seen, without property, they were taken into the
family of Thomas Ewing, by whom also William
T. was appointed to a cadetship at West Point.

IX

We have seen that the mental activity now known as "boosting" was assiduously practiced in the interest of western lands even before the colonies became independent. In fact, it may be said to have been set in motion by Columbus. We have already recorded some of its effects. It would almost seem as if there had been from the earliest times a number of men who were trying to depopulate the "East." And "the end is not yet."

In 1803 a Reverend Mr. Harris, a Massachusetts clergyman, visited Athens. He records that it is "situated on the Great Hocking River about forty miles by water from the Ohio, in the election district of Middletown." This Middletown was or was intended to be located somewhere on the river near the spot where the Hocking Valley railroad crosses it and where the earliest ferry to the west or northwest crossed it. "The town is regularly laid out on elevated ground of easy ascent round which the river flows in a graceful curve." What the reverend gentleman meant, if he correctly understood "the lay of the land," is that Athens is situated on a tract, some of which is fairly elevated and some quite low, round which the river flows—with a circumbendibus—somewhat in the form of a horseshoe, little of which, however, was a part of the town, strictly speaking, and a considerable portion of which will probably never be built upon. "The situation is healthy and the prospect delightful beyond description. The town is abundantly supplied with never-failing springs

[120]

of water and the adjacent country is thought to be
superior to any for pleasantness and fertility."
The epithet "Great," when applied to the Hocking
River, is a violent hyperbole, seeing that in many
places between Athens and the Ohio it is trans-
versely navigable "for boots" in dry seasons. Perhaps the author of the figure of speech wanted to
emphasize the disparity between the Great and the
Little Hocking, in view of the fact that it wends
its winding way across three counties, while its
small brother confines its meanderings to one a few
miles farther eastward. It would be interesting to
know which of the half-dozen curves the river makes
in getting around Athens the reverend gentleman
considered "graceful." Probably his imagination
supplied what was lacking in reality. One of the
curves was made by the apparent endeavor of the
current to flow up hill when the water is high. At
such times its course was straight but not strait.
The State Hospital authorities put an end to those
meandering vagaries by cutting, or rather by dig-
ging, a channel across the peninsula around which
the river usually made its way. The tenth of November, 1923, gave to our river an importance hitherto unsuspected by all persons except special students of American history. Henceforth it will no
longer be unhonored, although it seems to be still
unsung. On the above-named date, with ceremonies
that were at least elaborate if not imposing, representatives of the Daughters of the American Revolution unveiled a monument on the site of Fort
Gower where our clergyman's Great River mingles
its waters with the Ohio, which is never called
"great," in order to commemorate the first decla-

ration of American independence (1773). If the god of the river—according to the ancient Greeks every river has its god—had become almost disheartened by the long waiting of about one hundred and forty years, ample amends were made by giving to it its deserved place among the "records of the past." Albeit, three half centuries are not a long period in the annals of a river.

Perhaps the site reminded the original nomenclator of ancient Athens with its Acropolis and its Areopagus. Nor was he far astray. It would be interesting to know how it came about that so much of the old world, figuratively speaking, was spread over Athens County. What memories such names awaken in the minds of those to whom they speak an intelligible language—Athens, Alexander, Bern, Canaan, Carthage, Dover, Lodi, Rome, Troy, Waterloo and York. Of the fourteen townships constituting Athens County, two only or possibly three have home-grown names—Ames, Lee, and Trimble. The first of these is that of an early settler; the last, that of one of Ohio's governors. Both are mentioned elsewhere in this volume. The Hocking is a very human river. It is crooked, unreliable and lazy. Its sinuosities are so numerous that they have never been counted. Nobody knows months in advance what it will do next. It lies in its bed most of the time and comes out only when boosted by its little neighbors on both sides.

The city is connected with the surrounding country by five bridges, two of which are for the use of railroads only, although it can be entered by several different roads without crossing the river. At its southwestern corner the college campus approaches so close to the stream that there is little more than room enough for a street and a railroad. This road, the Baltimore and Ohio, was originally intended to pass under the town and a great deal of work was done in excavating a tunnel and building a "causeway." But owing to some legal requirement the track was laid, temporarily, as it was supposed, around, or at least around part of the town, and has never been moved. The history of railroad building into and through Athens is short but rather stormy. Its brevity is striking evidence of the newness of the oldest portion of the inhabited Northwest Territory. What is known as the Baltimore and Ohio railroad was built as the Marietta and Cincinnati. The first train reached Athens in the spring of 1856. Its arrival was a gala day in the village. But soon trouble developed between the officials of the road and the citizens of Athens and the county. Lawsuit after lawsuit was one of the results. The road lost money from the start, or rather it never made any to lose. The loss fell on the stockholders, many of whom not only in Athens County but all along the line were financially ruined. The road did not begin to pay until it was connected with the Baltimore and Ohio at Parkersburg, where it crosses the Ohio River on one of the first built and finest railroad bridges in the country. It was, however, and still is a private affair. It has withstood many an ice-jam and more floods, without suffering the slightest damage. The first train on the Hocking Valley road reached Athens, its southern, or rather its southeastern terminus, in 1870. The Kanawha and Michigan is of still later date. The railroads were preceded by a canal from Columbus, but which was abandoned several years ago. No one seems to know why it ended in an open field. The hospital grounds, although not within the limits of the municipality and notwithstanding the somewhat somber reflections it awakens, add not a little to the amenities of the environs. The college grounds are one block from the center of the city but far from its geographical center. The college buildings occupy somewhat more than the southern half; the remainder has been planted with trees; among them were a few that belonged to the original forest, which have, however, recently disappeared, owing to the infirmities of age. Lack of room compelled the college authorities to erect some of their largest buildings and more of the smaller ones outside of the original ten acres. The athletic ground and some of the experimental gardens lie outside of the corporation, occupying a tract of land between the southwest corner of the campus and the aforementioned hospital. The college also owns land east of the campus. The trustees of Miami University, which is one of the two original land-grant colleges or universities, were wiser or at least more prescient. They have a campus covering sixty acres of level land and will therefore have sufficient room for expansion, probably for all time. It may be noted, in this connection, that Dickinson College long ago found itself "cribbed, cabined, and confined," and was compelled to occupy land that was not in the original purchase from the heirs of William Penn. We meet the same conditions, that is the same state of mind, almost everywhere in the early history of our country. Not only did "the Fathers" have no idea of the expansion of colleges and of universities; they felt sure that the Mississippi River would be, for all time to come, not only the western limit of the United States but even of civilization. There is a very desirable location both for a large town and a college campus a few miles northwest of the present site of both, but its distance from the center of the township put it out of consideration. Here we have a practical illustration of what is meant by bringing the mountain to Mahomet. Twentieth-century Athens is a fine city with about ten thousand permanent and transient inhabitants living or sojourning within a mile of the courthouse. This estimate also includes the personnel of the state hospital, some of which is Athenian only by proximity and friendly intercourse. But its charm is chiefly artificial. Like the Roman citizenship of the chief captain mentioned in Acts, it was bought with a great price. The terrain somewhat resembles a huge toad squatting with its tail, figuratively speaking, against the Hocking and its head toward the northeast. There is considerable cultivable land on both sides of the river, but as has just been pointed out, some of it is low-lying and as the stream is very crooked it overflows its banks and becomes wider than the valley. Several times during the life of the present generation it has shown that it is no respector of property and once, its indifference to human life. Until recently some of the streets of Athens were of small value for traffic, while a few points within the corporation are accessible by means of ladders only or by means of other mountain-climbing devices. These drawbacks have, however, been mostly cancelled by the use of high-powered automobiles. Howbeit, there is still some level land within the corporation and more in sight; but there is also some in sight that is better suited for a kangaroo pasture than for quadrupeds whose legs are about of equal length. It is hard for us twentieth centurions to understand how the Athens of the preceding century could have been regularly laid out; for although some of the streets are straight laterally they are far from being so *flaterally*. By the end of the year 1800 about half a dozen widely scattered cabins constituted the village of Athens. At that time the population of Cincinnati was less than a thousand souls, Athens being the third municipality to be incorporated within the Northwest Territory, Ohio being not yet a State. Marietta preceded it by about three weeks. Here we see already the proclivity for incorporating prospects rather than realities, a penchant which prompted a native journalist to declare, "once upon a time" that his State engendered more politics to the square inch than any other in the Union. The more municipalities, the more mayors and other officials. That most of these—the offices no less than their incumbents including the villages—were mere pigmies mattered and still matters little. The governor of Delaware is as much a governor as the chief magistrate of New York or of California, despite the fact that his reign extends over but three counties. The governor of Nevada has at least more territory, if he has fewer subjects. To a person who is not "up" in statistics the mayor of Crooksburg or of Straighttown is as important a person as His Honor of Cleveland or Cincinnati.

The founders of Athens do not seem to have had

very large expectations of its future growth; otherwise they would not have laid out a "God's Acre" within about three blocks of the center and only one block farther from the college campus. Although fairly rapid from the times the increase of the population was only moderate. Here are some of the figures. In 1800 Washington County, which included Athens, was occupied by 5,427 people. Ten years later the population of Athens County was 2,787. In 1820 the population of Athens village was 729 and of the township 970 additional. In 1830 Athens township had a population of 1,054 and Ames 721. The population of Nelsonville was less than a hundred. The first postoffice in Athens was put in operation in January, 1804, although it was not, strictly speaking, in the village, but on the right bank of the Hocking River east of the town. A few months later it was transferred to a building in Athens. The small amount of mail was carried overland on horseback. For almost twenty years there was only one postoffice in Athens County, when another was established in Ames township. From Wheeling to Cincinnati the mail was carried in small boats each way. What was destined for Athens was deposited at Marietta.

If Diogenes were to visit the Athens (O.) of the present century he could find many honest men without lighting his lantern. He could find others who are honest when and as long as it paid to be honest. He would also find some who made no pretense to be honest. "A fellow has got to live."

X

The government of American colleges, especially of those that have expanded into universities, presents one of those strange contrasts to be met with everywhere in our social fabric. As the country gradually passed from a republic into a democracy the authority of their presidents became increasingly autocratic. This was due to the fact demonstrated by experience that it was the most feasible plan. In the very nature of the case a board of trustees cannot "run" a college, or anything else in fact, except by delegating their authority to a small number of men, generally to one. Wherever they have tried to do so they have failed. Now and then a corrupt or inefficient president has wrought harm, but it has rarely been serious or irreparable. It is not only true that the best government is an autocracy, if the autocrat is wise, enlightened and unselfish; it is equally true of a college that it is most efficient and achieves most nearly the object for which it was founded if its destinies are presided over and directed by an enlightened autocrat. Autocrat and despot or tyrant are not interchangeable terms. At the best, there are doubtless acts of injustice done, but they are probably far fewer than under a regime in which side-issues and personal interests have more or less free play. Thomas Jefferson introduced his democratic ideas into the institution of which he was the founder, and for about three-fourths of a century the University of Virginia seems to have done fairly well. But the time arrived when it was found to be essential or

[128]

at least desirable to choose a president; and there
does not seem to be any serious movement in favor
of a return to former conditions. Quite recently
the trustees of one of our largest and most populous
universities decided, for some reason, that they
could dispense with a president. But a brief experience taught them their error and they returned to
their former status. It is almost impossible for a
board of trustees to have a policy, certainly not a
wise policy. If their term of office is too long they
fall behind the age; if too short, they are prone to
be misled by fads that are equally liable to do harm.
Moreover, not all boards are alike, or even similar
synchronously throughout the country; nor is the
board that is the same in law always the same in
fact; hence praise and blame are certain to be deserved somewhere. In fact, most boards are now
and then subjected to criticism, not always unde-
servedly. A distinguished American engineer is said
to have remarked, on a certain occasion, that after
considerable experience with boards he had found
some of them to be long, narrow and thin, and
occasionally crooked. There are several hundred
boards of college trustees in the country. It is
probable that most of their members were and are
wise according to their lights—would anybody deny
that some of them were otherwise? The president of a city university in Ohio once remarked
to the writer that "our board will talk and wran-
gle for an hour about the payment of a bill
of five dollars, then vote away hundreds of dollars almost without discussion." It was reported
some years ago that when a new professor was
to be chosen, in a certain college, not in Ohio,

the president of the board suggested that the vacancy be filled by the lowest bidder. Howbeit, the writer, after considerable study of conditions in Europe, became convinced that on the whole there is less injustice done in American institutions of higher learning than anywhere else in the world. The "bulldozing" of German professors by the government is largely responsible for the chaotic conditions now prevailing in the Vaterland. In a few pages of Wells' "Outlines of History," under the caption of "The Catastrophe of Modern Imperialism," the reader will find graphically described the methods by which German education was not only directed but driven towards the attainment of the most ignoble and unattainable ends. If we are prone to find fault with one thing because it is not another, we shall be in a constant state of obtrectation. There is probably more room for and need of improvement in our public schools than in our institutions of higher learning. The question whether a college education "pays" is being answered in the affirmative by a large number of our young people. Perhaps it would be better to write "going to college," as the college of the twentieth century has many attractions besides history, science, literature and the fine arts. Unfortunately, many of our students expect to reap a bountiful harvest from inferior soil, poorly cultivated and sown or planted with untested seed. They usually discover their mistake, but not always in time to correct it. Students not a few spend more time and labor in trying to conceal their ignorance than would be required to remove it. On the other hand, there is a long list of names of men who made a poor undergraduate record and a notable record in after life. To confuse the situation still more, many of our men of note never went to college. Some of them can hardly be said to have gone to school at all. We are therefore justified in saying to our boys and young men: If you are quite sure that you are endowed with exceptional abilities, that is if you are a genius, it makes little difference how you spend your time, provided you do not spend it in idleness or vice. And remember too that a college is no place for geniuses. As most of us who teach and nearly all the young people who go to college are "ordinary folk," none of us is wise if we waste our time. Without doubt we are a thousand times better informed than were the Athenians of twenty-five centuries ago, but it is a question whether we are wiser, if wisdom consist in making the best possible use of our knowledge. "Knowledge comes but wisdom lingers." *We,* when used in this connection, means the people of western Europe and their descendants. An instructive parellel might be drawn between the causes that led to the destruction of the Athenian empire, and the downfall of Germany in our day. Inordinate ambition and the lust of conquest was responsible for both catastrophes. If we are wiser it is because we have profited by experience and only to the extent that we have profited. Sir Henry Sumner Maine has left upon record the dictum: "Everything that moves except the blind forces of nature is due to the Greeks." Sir Francis Galton was of the opinion that the average ability of the Athenian race is, at the lowest possible estimate, very nearly two degrees higher than our own, that is, about as much as our race is above the negro.

We are not responsible for our inherent inferiority;
we are responsible for the use we make of our increased knowledge and of our far greater opportunities. It is instructive to note that the twentieth-
century interest in athletics is a return to an ancient
Greek ideal, although in this matter the British have
long preceded us. All knowledge is due to curiosity; but curiosity, unless wisely directed, leads to
nothing and to nowhere. To St. Paul, with his
oriental mind, the Athenians, with their lively interest in every new thing, was a strange phenome-
non. Howbeit, Athenian curiosity in his day had
degenerated into mere childishness. It is reported
of R. W. Emerson that when he was once asked by
a young man where he should go to school and what
he should study, answered: "It does not matter
much what you study or where; what matters is
how you study and with whom." One thing we may
take for granted: If the respondent to the question:
"Where were you educated?" names any particular
time or place his education is defective. There is
only one proper answer to such a question: "Wherever I have been since I was ten years old." In
our time there is so much knowledge worth acquir-
ing—which does not mean that it is being put into
print—that no wise man will say that he was educated at any place or in any particular period of
his life. When Socrates, in his seventieth year, was
in prison awaiting his execution, he said to his
visiting friends: "In the days gone by we have dis-
cussed many profound problems and have reached
definite conclusions. But if you think we were in
error, in any particular I am willing to go over
them again and to change my mind, if shown that

[132]

we were in error." How many men in our day who are equally advanced in years would be willing to admit that some of their beliefs and opinions were erroneous?

This modest volume closes with the wish that every one who reads it will endeavor, in however small a degree,

-to render less
The sum of human wretchedness
And more, its sum of blessedness.

He is the greatest who confers the most benefits.

By the same Author

A PIONEER COLLEGE AND ITS BACKGROUND

(DICKINSON)

[133]